The Go

The Good Life

Ethics and the Pursuit of Happiness

Herbert McCabe OP

Edited and Introduced by Brian Davies OP

B L O O M S B U R Y

LONDON • NEW DELHI • NEW YORK • SYDNEY

A Continuum Book
Bloomsbury Publishing Plc
50 Bedford Square
London WC1B 3DP

www.bloomsbury.com

Bloomsbury Publishing, London, New Delhi,
New York and Sydney

First published 2012

© The Estate of Herbert McCabe 2005

A CIP record for this book is available from the British Library

ISBN 978-0-8264-7647-0

Contents

Introduction

Herbert McCabe (who died in 2001) has now managed to publish as many books since his death as he did in his lifetime. While vigorous and active, he produced *The New Creation* (1964), *Law, Love and Language* (1968) and *God Matters* (1987).[1] At the time of his death, however, he left much unpublished material behind, and I am privileged to have been able to work some of it up so as to see the light of day. In 2002, therefore, Herbert gave us *God Still Matters*.[2] And in 2003 we got *God, Christ and Us*.[3] Both of these volumes have received critical acclaim – unsurprisingly so since Herbert was one of the sharpest minds of his generation and also a very readable author (he was a fan of G. K. Chesterton, P. G. Wodehouse and Jane Austen, and their stylistic influence on him is apparent in his writings).

The present book is Herbert's third posthumous offering. And it deals with issues which concerned him greatly but were not especially focused on in *God Still Matters* and *God, Christ and Us*. Though a distinguished philosopher, Herbert was also an influential theologian, and those volumes chiefly (though not exclusively) reflect his lifelong preoccupation with God, and with Christ as God's way of bringing us to share in the divine life. So, with a

1 First published by Sheed and Ward (London), *Law, Love and Language* was reprinted by Continuum (London and New York) in 2003. *The New Creation* was published by Sheed and Ward, London. *God Matters* was published by Geoffrey Chapman, London.
2 Herbert McCabe, *God Still Matters* (Continuum, London and New York, 2002).
3 Herbert McCabe, *God, Christ and Us* (Continuum, London and New York, 2003).

few exceptions, their chapters home in on those concerns (continually drawing attention to, for example, the difference between God and creatures, the involvement of God in our world, and ways in which we might conform ourselves to God's eternal plan for our well-being – while reflecting on what we are doing when trying to do that).[4] Yet Herbert's thoughts on God naturally led him to thoughts about what it is to be human. And he therefore had a sustained interest in ethical questions. What does it mean to call something (or someone) good? Are there ethical truths? If so, where are they to be found? Can we argue about ethics? Are there good and bad ways of thinking about how people should behave? If so, how are we to distinguish between them? To what extent does an understanding of what people are generate ethical conclusions? Can there be sensible and important ethical thinking which is not explicitly governed by theological presuppositions? Can one be sound on morals without believing in God? Questions like these always fascinated Herbert, and in this book we find him tackling them head on.

I should explain that what follows is best described as a work in progress rather than a finished product. As I went through his literary remains it became clear to me that Herbert had been planning another book on ethics (in succession to *Law, Love and Language*). He even had a preface written (published in what follows). But he clearly did not complete the book, which is much to be regretted. What he finished writing, however, is well worth reading, and I am therefore grateful to Continuum for agreeing to

---

4 In *God Still Matters* the exceptions are Chapter 7 ('Christ and Politics'), Chapter 13 ('Sense and Sensibility'), Chapter 14 ('Aquinas on Good Sense'), and Chapter 17 ('Teaching Morals').

publish what we might regard as parts of an unhappily unfinished greater project. When going through Herbert's papers I found two unpublished articles ('Virtue and Truth' and 'Animals and Us') which expand on ideas touched on in this incomplete work. So these are also included in the present volume.

Readers should not be misled by what I said in the last paragraph but one. They should never suppose that Herbert McCabe ever drew a sharp distinction between (a) thinking about God and Christ, and (b) thinking about what is good for people (thinking about ethics or morality). For him, people are God's creatures, and what is good for them cannot be something without theological implications. But, like Thomas Aquinas (1224/6–74), to whom he owed a huge intellectual debt, Herbert thought that there are sound ways of thinking about what we do which can be argued for without special reference to any particular religious belief (e.g. that God exists). He defends this claim in *Law, Love and Language*, and he continues to do so in what follows. So, though it makes reference to theological themes, this new book is very much a work of philosophy. Appealing to reason, it develops an approach to action. In *God Matters* Herbert wrote: 'Most argument in morals is an appeal to intellectual honesty and the great test of intellectual honesty is logical coherence.'[5] All of Herbert's writings display such honesty and coherence, and the present work applies it to moral questions.

I should, perhaps, stress that Herbert always thought of ethics with a serious eye on rigorous argument. He never thought of moral judgements as mere expressions of attitude or taste. He thought of them as able to have truth

5 *God Matters*, p. 200.

value and, therefore, as open to thoughtful debate. Aquinas distinguishes between theoretical reasoning (reasoning about what is the case) and practical reasoning (reasoning about what to do). He also argues that one can make intellectual mistakes when engaging in both these kinds of reasoning. And Herbert was of the same mind. So his ethical thinking is very much concerned to reach conclusions that any right-thinking person would want to reach. In this sense, it is thoroughly objectivist. But it differs strikingly from a number of other objectivist approaches to ethics. Some of these drive a wedge between facts and values – arguing that ethical conclusions cannot be deduced from purely factual premises. An interesting aspect of Herbert's ethical objectivism is that it challenges this distinction between facts and values. Aquinas holds that we know what is the case only in so far as we want to pay attention to (value paying attention to) certain things. He also maintains that value judgements (e.g. 'X is good') reflect both desires and attitudes to facts on the part of those who make them. Herbert takes up such points in his own thinking. So he draws attention to ways in which moral judgements can be argued for and deemed to be true (or false) while also stressing that they are not purely cerebral but also engage with our wants and needs. When he was teaching at Oxford he gave an introductory course on moral philosophy (mostly he lectured on Aquinas). He called the course 'How to be Happy'. This title pretty much sums up his approach to ethics, which is well exemplified in the present volume.

How original is this approach? You could say 'Not very'. For (as Herbert often noted, and as he emphasizes below) it is very much present in the writings of Aristotle

(384–322 BC) and Aquinas. But the ethical ideas they champion pretty much went underground among moral philosophers (mainstream ones, anyway) round about the sixteenth century. So Herbert's approach to ethics is, in a way, original. But, as he was also delighted to note (and as he also emphasizes below), it is one which has undergone a serious revival in the last thirty years or so. Once again, therefore, one might view it as unoriginal. But, of course, the most important question to ask about it is 'Is it right?' And readers, I think, will find that, if their answer is 'Yes' they will also want to say that Herbert McCabe had a highly personal way of showing that this is so. He was one of the most intelligent people I have ever met, and his intelligence shows on every page of his ethical writings. He had a clarity and directness rare amongst moral philosophers (rare, indeed, amongst philosophers in general). And he had an engaging way of helping one to see why one is right even if, on reflection, one finds his conclusions obvious (and, in that sense, unoriginal). The well-known contemporary moral theologian Stanley Hauerwas says of him: 'His argument is so elegant and his examples so apposite that one might be tempted to miss how he is trying to help us avoid theory-driven mistakes that make it impossible for us to see what is right before our eyes.'[6] Hauerwas is here obliquely alluding to the work of Ludwig Wittgenstein (1889–1951), arguably the greatest of twentieth-century philosophers, one famous for conceiving of philosophy as the task of assembling certain kinds of reminders. He sees the philosopher as one who tries to look

---

6 Hauerwas wrote this in a Foreword intended for the 2003 reprint of *Law, Love and Language*. Unfortunately, the publisher omitted to include this Foreword in the published volume.

and see what is there for all to observe – and therefore as being seriously unoriginal.[7] But it sometimes (as in the case of Wittgenstein) takes an original mind to draw attention to the obvious. And Herbert McCabe certainly had such a mind – one displayed in what he says about ethics (but also in what he says on other topics).

Wittgenstein, by the way, was a definite influence on Herbert's thinking, including his ethical thinking. And here we come to another aspect of Herbert's ethical originality. For, as I have noted, much of what he says about ethics is indebted to Aquinas, and there are not many Thomist ethicists who also draw on Wittgenstein. People who like Aquinas's ethical writings tend to read them in isolation from the work of other philosophers (especially those who might be placed in what is sometimes called 'the analytical tradition'). But Herbert never read Aquinas in isolation. He thought of him as an ongoing partner in discussion, one to bring into conversations with the best of thinkers regardless of where they come from intellectually. So he made Aquinas converse with Wittgenstein as few with a respect for Aquinas have done.[8] He chiefly did so by focusing on language and by taking much that Aquinas says about knowing and thinking to anticipate what, in various places, Wittgenstein says about meaning and understanding. Some Thomistic purists will not

7 See Ludwig Wittgenstein, *Philosophical Investigations* (translated by G. E. M. Anscombe, Basil Blackwell, Oxford, 1968), §127 and following.

8 Two other figures (both of them friends of Herbert) who have done the same are Anthony Kenny and David Burrell. See, for example, Anthony Kenny. *Aquinas on Mind* (Routledge, London and New York, 1993) and David Burrell, *Aquinas, God and Action* (Routledge and Kegan Paul, London and Henley, 1979).

approve of Herbert in this respect. Yet as he often asked: 'Was Aquinas ever a Thomist?' The question (always intended rhetorically by Herbert) was meant to insist that Aquinas never thought of himself as the last word on anything – that he saw himself as a voice in a discussion, one concerned to listen as well as to teach. Herbert's ability to present Aquinas as such a voice (as he does in the present book) was one of his greatest gifts.[9]

Brian Davies OP
Fordham University
New York

9 I am grateful to Fordham University, New York, for awarding me time to prepare the present volume for publication. I am also grateful to Michael Moreland for proofreading assistance.

Preface

If readers discover any new truths in the course of reading this book, they should not attribute this to any originality of mine. That will be exhibited only in my mistakes. For my aim in what follows is simply to expound, as faithfully and sympathetically as I can, a certain tradition of ethical thinking, one which is particularly well expressed in the *philosophical* account that Thomas Aquinas (c. 1225–1274) gives of human behaviour. I stress the word 'philosophical' here because, although most of my quotations from Aquinas will be from his works of theology, he thought that there is much to say about ethics even in abstraction from any faith in divine revelation. And his work is, in great part, one particular development of a tradition going back to the pagan Aristotle (384–322 BC).

This book is meant to be an elementary introduction. So I have dealt a great deal in approximations and have not, for example, mentioned many subtle refinements that make Aquinas one of the greatest of thinkers. Thus, for instance, I have throughout treated thinking as more or less synonymous with talking (whether to others or to oneself) while Aquinas does not explicitly write as though he agrees with me on this issue. But taking him as doing so helps one to a good first approximation of his doctrine, which I even sometimes advocate in what follows without mentioning him at all. You should treat my text as a tourist map of what may be to you, and certainly is to many, an unfamiliar piece of intellectual territory – a map offered by someone who finds the landscape congenial. What I have written here contains other simplifications that may trouble the experts. But this book is not written for them.

It will become evident that my debt is not only to Aquinas but also to a certain kind of modern interpreter. Once, largely through the work of Wittgenstein (1889–1951), the centuries-long domination of Western thinking by Cartesian and related empiricist doctrines had been broken, it became possible for philosophers to look back with a fresh understanding to pre-Cartesian thinking, in particular to Aquinas, and to discover how very congenial so much of his writing is to modern styles of questioning and answering. So I have been able to borrow shamelessly from Wittgenstein himself, but also from Elizabeth Anscombe (1919–2001), Peter Geach, Philippa Foot, Anthony Kenny, Alasdair MacIntyre and Gilbert Ryle (1900–1976) – though, perhaps, they (those of them still living at any rate) would not all acknowledge, or even recognize, their insights in the simplifications to which they have been reduced. This also means that what I have to say will sometimes seem strange to the older kind of 'Thomist' who was, I believe, often unwittingly influenced by empiricist or Cartesian presuppositions. So responses to my reflections and expositions are likely to take the form of arguments from many sides. But what other reason is there for writing any philosophical book?

Herbert McCabe OP

1

The Study of (Ethics)

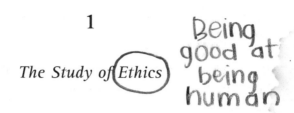

Being good at being human

In this book I want, among other things, to talk about the way we praise or blame other people and ourselves, about the way we think of some people as good and others as not so good. So I am concerned with ethics. And I start from the presupposition that praising and blaming is a perfectly sensible activity, that it is not like predicting the future from the dimensions of the great pyramid, or seeking to cure diphtheria by incantations at the time of the full moon, or hoping to defend your country by the use of nuclear weapons (all of which belong to the realm of magic rather than rationality). Praising and blaming (especially blaming) can be carried to excess or indulged in inappropriately. For now, though, I take it that they are ordinary and necessary human activities.

We may know reasonably well how to praise and blame without studying ethics – just as we may speak quite grammatically without every having studied grammar. But the study of ethics, like that of grammar, is useful for at least two reasons. First, it is always satisfactory to see the reasons and principles and patterns behind what we do. Secondly, even though we speak quite grammatically for the most part, there may be times when we make mistakes or are puzzled about some linguistic form. And a study of grammar will help us to avoid mistakes in these cases. It might lead us to see that, if we are to be consistent with our own general practice, it is *this* we should say and not *that*. By the same token, the norms of traditional morality, like those of grammar, are never stable, and never quite adequate to deal with new forms of human behaviour. So we need some way of determining what is a growth in our understanding and what is merely a decay, what, in the case of grammar, is a new and linguistic form, and what is mere slovenliness.

I do not want to carry the comparison between ethics and grammar any further than that, for it could be misleading in several ways. For instance, it is quite clear that what are perfectly acceptable grammatical forms now were once grammatical errors (not just *thought to be*, but actually *were*) and vice versa. The grammar of a language changes constantly and without undue fuss, and it is nothing like so clear that our judgements of praise and blame change so quickly, though they undoubtedly do change. That is another reason for looking into ethics. There have been obvious changes (especially in the last hundred years or so) in the way we praise and blame people with regard to animals, women, torture, wealth, weapons, sex, punishment, and lots of other things. If we are to decide rationally which of these changes are to be welcomed and which resisted, we shall need to look into the principles that we employ in coming to judgements of this kind.

In what follows I shall be speaking in one definite tradition of ethical thinking, because so far as I can see this is the only tradition (in its manifold variations) that makes rational sense of our ethical judgements. I think that alternative approaches sooner or later make ethical judgements irrational – not in the sense of bad or wrong, but simply in the sense that they are not decidable by thinking or argument. You are reduced to saying something like: 'Well, that's your view. Mine is different. We shall just have to agree to differ.' That is often a very sensible thing to say about judgements of particular matters where there is not enough common ground or enough information to argue the case either way. It is not, I think, a sensible thing to say about *every* ethical judgement. It is not at all clear how an ethical judgement *could be* nothing but a personal view. I mean: why would it count as an ethical *judgement* rather than simply a cry of rage or delight? There have been philosophers who held that ethical judgements just *are* more or less disguised cries of rage or delight, that they do not tell us anything about the value of the behaviour or persons they purport to be about, that they just show us how the speaker feels. This philosophical position is, for me, ruled out by my presupposition that praising and blaming is a sensible human activity; for if all you want to do is express your rage or delight it seems to me sensible to do it with four-letter words or whoops of joy rather than disguising it misleadingly in what look like statements of truth. This, as I understand him, is what Nietzsche (1844–1900) thought. If what you are concerned to do is exercise your will as power, have the honesty not to disguise it in moralistic terms.

In the tradition from which I speak, which we may call the tradition of Aristotle, understood with the help of Aquinas, it is thought proper to praise those actions and dispositions that lead to and are *constitutive* of that human satisfaction in which happiness consists. In other words, for this tradition, the notion of human satisfaction and happiness is a basic one, though not an *obvious* one. We need to distinguish this way of looking at ethics from that of those who see the basic principles as *right* or *law*, who say we should praise those who do what is commanded and refrain from what is forbidden. But perhaps more immediately we need to distinguish it from what is called 'utilitarianism' – the view that we should praise every act (or sometimes every type of act) that leads to the greatest happiness of the greatest number. I say there is a more immediate need for distinguishing here, because there is most likely to be confusion. The difference, however, is expressed in that word 'constitutive'. For the Aristotelian, happiness is not just the *result* of praiseworthy action; it is *constituted by* virtuous action. The Utilitarian praises an action or type of action because of the *consequences* he expects from it. The Aristotelian praises it for *what it is in itself* – in some way a *constituent* of human satisfaction and happiness.

The Aristotelian tradition does not reject the ideas of right, rights, or law, but puts them in a secondary place. They have their validity and necessity within, and only within, the quest for human excellence or satisfaction. It is because such satisfaction requires community, and because community requires law and rights, that we praise those who obey the law. Community is not founded upon law; rather, law is founded upon community. What community is founded upon is friendship as a necessary part of human satisfaction.

It is an important difference between an Aristotelian and a Utilitarian that for the Utilitarian happiness is an empirically identifiable state, one which is simply recognized by being experienced and one which, as the most desirable state, it is rational to seek by various means to maximize. Happiness for him is first of all an experience. For the Aristotelian, on the other hand, happiness is fundamentally an activity; it is the state of the person who is living without hindrance the life that becomes a human being, the 'satisfactory' life (the life 'sufficiently made'). Happiness is not like, say, pain, the name of an experience any more than, say, friendship is. We learn how to use words like 'happiness' and 'friendship' in much more complex ways than we learn how to use 'pain'. It would be at least peculiar for a man to be mistaken about whether he was in pain a few minutes ago, whereas the Aristotelian thinks a person may easily think she is happy or living in friendship when she is not. For example, what she takes for her friendship may be a form of selfishness which she does not recognize precisely *because* of the vice from which she suffers. For part of what is meant by a bad man is one who is so self-deluded that he wants and seeks and regards as his happiness what is not in fact true happiness. So if we want to know what is that 'satisfactory' life, 'life that is becoming to a human being' (so that we can know what true happiness is), it won't do simply to ask everybody, including ourselves, what they think they want most. We shall have to ask only the good people, for the rest will be more or less deluded.

But how do we recognize the good people? They are those who live as becomes a human being. There is a circle here; but is it a vicious one? It might be but for one other factor: we ourselves who are asking the questions have both our perceptions and our delusions; our perceptions in so far as we have, or struggle towards, virtue; our delusions in so far as we settle for vice. A totally vicious, and thus totally deluded, person cannot study ethics. It is only with the learning and acquisition of virtue that we begin to recognize the good man or woman.

The thing is, however, not totally black or white. Not all giving in to evil implies total blindness. We can know, at least in the early stages, what we are about. We can recognize and admire the good person even as we know that we are not much like her. This is a point of insertion into the 'hermeneutical circle' or dialectic of ethics. We recognize some good people, we know some of the things that they aim at and see as good; in this way we can begin to formulate a notion of 'the life that is becoming to a human being', the 'good life' for short, and with this notion we can come back and re-appraise both ourselves and our perceptions and also the life of those we saw as in many respects good.

I say this is one point of insertion into the circle: 'Good men are those who have appropriate goals, appropriate goals are those that good men have.' But it is by no means our only or our most important point. Our moral perceptions and judgements, like all our other judgements, begin not from our own bare experience, but from the society and tradition into which we are born and in which we are brought up. It is important to see what is meant by this upbringing. It is not simply a matter of learning certain theoretical truths. It is not just a matter of handing on certain propositions such as might have been recorded in a book. It is a training in what Aristotle would call the practical intellect, the appetites, and even the perceptions. It is not just learning that certain things are the case; it is also learning to want some things rather than others, to enjoy some things rather than others, and it is learning to behave reasonably in view of these wants. So it is a training of the moral understanding. By 'moral understanding', I do not mean any mysterious intuition or 'moral sense'. I just mean that we come to recognize, say, a generous act as praiseworthy just as we come to recognize a particular move in football or ice-skating as excellent. None of these recognitions simply comes naturally. They are all the result of education.

For Aristotle, you might say, ethics is the study of education, which means, amongst other things, that ethics is the study of how it becomes possible to study ethics. (Aristotle was not, of course, original in this. For Plato [c. 427–347 BC] in the *Republic*, and even more emphatically in the *Laws*, ethics is about *paideia*, education.) Only the educated person, the one who has learnt how to be good at being human, the virtuous person, is in a position clearly to recognize virtue for what it is. Of course 'education' here means something that only occasionally overlaps with the modern concept of education (which has mostly to do with having read the right books). For the Aristotelian, the educated person is one who has acquired the virtues – though, as we shall see, there are intellectual virtues that are sometimes at least as important as the moral ones.

So we begin our study of ethics as recipients from our tradition of some understanding of the good life – just as we begin the study of grammar as recipients of a tradition of speaking grammatically. One of the things we shall have to look at is how such a tradition and education is possible. How could we *teach* people to be good? Another thing we should look at is how it might become (and, perhaps, *is* becoming) impossible. We live, after all, in a society whose predominant ideology or theory of itself is that

9

there is not, or should not be, any such tradition. The conventional wisdom is that it is no business of society to interfere with or influence anybody's morals — this is a matter purely for the individual conscience. Society, says the conventional wisdom, exists to protect us from each other, to keep the peace between people with quite divergent views of the good life. This is the theoretical foundation or *credo* of the secular or liberal society: society is a peaceful coexistence of potential or real enemies. Friendship and love do not come within the purview of society as such. They are too personal and too sacred for the marketplace.

In my view, ethics still exists only because this liberal ideology misdescribes the society in which it grew up. Of course, all ideologies in some ways do this — but usually in the direction of making a society sound more pleasant than it really is. In this case, the liberal ideology is unfair to its world. There is, in fact, a great deal of shared moral belief and perception handed down in various groups within our society, although, because it is unrecognized or disowned or sentimentalized, it is undoubtedly being eroded. Thus, what an Aristotelian would recognize as education still does go on in homes, schools, churches, political groups, charitable organizations, and even to some extent in universities. Such a tradition can be the starting-point for establishing some understanding of the good life in terms of which we can reappraise and criticize the whole tradition we have received. Without such a living, critical response, tradition is lost and replaced by a static appeal to (or rejection of) the opinions and values of the immediate past. The tradition is not handed down simply in words. It is handed down in institutions and practices within society (all of which of course involve words). Our critical reception of the tradition is not, then, simply a matter of changing our words and ideas but of changing fundamental structures of human living. It is a political matter. What is done with, for example, a society's health resources, or its police force, amounts to a series of ethical statements concerning the good life.

What I have been saying so far is in the nature of a manifesto, and, like all manifestos, it has contained a good many question-begging phrases and scandalous assumptions. Philosophy, I think, and theology too, need manifestos. But philosophy and theology only begin when we start to look at them critically. So let us look at some of the dubious expressions I have used.

Take, to begin with, the phrase 'the life that is becoming to a human being'. This raises at least two questions: First, can we talk of the life that *is* becoming to a human being, as though this were a question of *fact*, as though the phrase 'the life that is becoming to a human being' should be thought of as comparable to an expression like 'the mushrooms that are poisonous to a human being'? Are we dealing in ethics with matters of first-level ascertainable truth?

By 'first-level truth' here I mean truth which is not just truth about people's opinions. Thus there are many important second-level truths (as we may call them) about people's beliefs about, say, the flatness of our planet. But there are no first-level truths about it since the earth just is not flat. So a philosopher or a sociologist might recognize that there are important second-level truths about people's beliefs in an objective moral order (in which some behaviour just is, in fact, becoming to a human being, and some is not). But the same philosopher or sociologist might also deny that there are any first-level truths about it since there does not exist any such objective moral order for there to be truths about. I shall be trying to convince you that there are not only second-level but also first-level truths about what is becoming to a human being: that in some respects the proposition 'Rape is a bad thing' resembles the proposition 'Some toadstools are poisonous'.

A second, and I think more difficult, question raised by the use of the phrase 'the life that is becoming to a human being' is whether we are entitled to that initial definite article: '*The* life that is ...' Is there just *one* such life to be discovered, the life that is becoming or appropriate (or 'non-poisonous') to just any human being simply in virtue of belonging to the human race, regardless of the society in which he or she was educated and the culture in which he or she was formed? This question will not arise for one who has already answered my first question in the negative. But suppose that we decide that moral propositions *are* first-level truths. In that case, my second question remains. Is our ethics to be grounded in the cultural life of people? And is it therefore a matter of what might be said of a *particular* historical culture? Or is to be grounded in humanity?

It seems possible to think of ethical propositions as both objective and relative. In other words, defending the objectivity of the good life does not commit you to defending the notion of 'natural law' – the idea that there are things becoming and unbecoming to human beings as such just in virtue of their nature, just in virtue of the kind of animals that they are. The idea of natural law depends, as I see it, on being somehow able to see humanity itself on the analogy of a society bound together in friendship. This notion is, I think, implicit in the Christian gospel. But it is not philosophically perspicuous.

The statement of the case for relativism has not, I think, been improved upon since Herodotus (in fifth-century Greece) penned the following words:

> Everyone without exception believes his own native customs, and the religion he was brought up in, to be the best; and that being so, it is unlikely that anyone but a madman would mock at such things. There is abundant evidence that this is the universal feeling about the ancient customs of one's country. One might recall, in particular, an anecdote of Darius. When he was king of Persia, he summoned the Greeks who happened to be present at his court, and asked them what they would take to eat the dead bodies of their fathers. They replied that they would not do it for any money in the world. Later, in the presence of the Greeks, and through an interpreter, so that they could understand what was said, he asked some Indians, of the tribe called Callatiae, who do in fact eat their parents' dead bodies, what they would take to burn them. They uttered a cry of horror and forbade him to mention such a dreadful thing. One can see by this what custom can do, and Pindar, in my opinion, was right when he called it 'king of all'.[1]

Herodotus's word for custom here is *ethos*, from which we get the word 'ethics', just as the equivalent Latin word for

---

1 Herodotus, *Histories* 3, 36–40.

custom (*mores*) gives us 'morals'. So the question arises: would not a rational ethics simply be the study of the customs of a particular culture or society? Would it not amount to pure anthropology? Within each society there would be praise or blame according to whether behaviour was or was not in accordance with traditional received customs. People would feel strongly about deviant behaviour because it would threaten the ancient structures of the society and thus represent a sinking into chaos. It would make sense then to make judgements within the terms of a particular society but no sense to judge transculturally between different traditions. There would be fairly clear objective judgements to be made in each society – ethics would not be subjective, a matter of expressing feelings and attitudes – but judgements would be relative: relative to that particular tradition and culture.

I shall be trying to convince you that there could be, and in fact are, valid transcultural moral judgements, that not all moral judgements are relative to some particular society. Of course I can know that what to me (in my society) are obligations will appear, from the perspective of another society, as contingent customs. And I can know that what appear to me as mere customs will be viewed as genuine obligations in other societies. But is that sort of thing *all* I can know when it comes to ethics? Maybe not. And in order to see why not, perhaps we can move to the question 'Can we speak of the behaviour which *is* becoming to a human being?'

2

The Good Life

Is there something to be *discovered* which is, in fact, the good life? Could I be *mistaken* about the character of the good life and describe it in mistaken ways? Are moral judgements really statements which may be true or false, or are they merely expressions of a speaker's desires and feelings? And is there really such a thing as *the* good life? Or is there merely the kind of life that I or someone else would *like* people to live?

I think that the view that moral judgements are not true or false but merely expressions of feelings or desire is one of those philosophical positions that nobody would hold unless she thought she had to, unless she thought that any alternative position must be untenable. It is held in the way that John Locke (1632–1704) held that secondary qualities, like colours, do not belong to physical objects, or the way that Aquinas held that God brings about my free actions.[1] Both these very implausible-sounding views were held because the apparently common-sense alternative was thought to be impossible. (The fact that in my view, whereas Locke's implausible view was wrong, Aquinas's was right, is neither here nor there for present purposes.)

---

1 For Locke, see *An Essay Concerning Human Understanding* (1689), Book II, Chapter VIII. For Aquinas, see *De Potentia*, 3,1.

The common-sense view, held by most people, and even most off-duty philosophers, is that we are saying something *true* if we say that imprisoning innocent people is wrong or that rape is wicked. People who deny these propositions, we think, are not just bad (and perhaps not even bad), but mistaken. People only come round to thinking of such apparent propositions as expressions of will (of, for example, a sheer desire to bring about a society without such activities as rape), because they have become convinced that badness or wrongness *could not* be a property or characteristic, part of the description of, human activity; it could not be something we *observe* or *discover* in the world. They have become convinced that to say that some action is bad is to compare it with what it ought to be, and that what something ought to be is not an object of our experience. They have become convinced that we only see what is there and that when we look at the world we can only see what *is* the case, not what *ought* to be but is not the case. And they think that there is no way of deducing what ought to be from what is. What is the case, the facts, can be stated truly, or else we can be mistaken about them; but whether something ought or ought not to be, its value, can only be something we aspire to or want, or can only be something that we know others want.

You might think that we can save the objective, factual status of values by claiming that *God* wants us to do certain things and not others. If values were simply a matter of *your* will or *mine*, they would be subjective and not a descriptive feature of things in the world. But, so someone might reason, since they are a matter of God's will, which is unchanging, we can make objective statements about values if we happen to know what it is that God wills. We would then mean by 'a bad action' 'something that God, as a matter of fact, wants us not to do, something that transgresses his commandment'. This would be an objective matter. It *is the case* that God does not want this done.

It would be an objective truth, however, at what I have called the second level. When we record that God does not want (has forbidden) some activity, we are speaking like the anthropologist who records that the Greeks did not want people to eat their dead parents. And nothing seems to follow from this about the nature of human activities in themselves, just as human activities. A view which would seek to make rational sense of ethical judgements simply in terms of the will or law of *God* is no less voluntarist than one which seeks to make sense of them in terms of *my* will. In neither case is any rightness or wrongness, goodness or badness, attributed to the human action because of what it is in itself.

So we seem left with, and thus compelled to, the view that it is one thing to give an account, a description, of what is the case, which, because it is 'value-free', will contain nothing but verifiable truths; and quite another human activity to speak of the moral value of this or that piece of behaviour: this latter does not tell us descriptive truths; it simply expresses the attitudes or options or feelings of the speaker, or, perhaps, of God. *Ought* (prescription) can never be derived from *is* (description). The classical statement of this conclusion comes from David Hume (1711–1776). In his *A Treatise of Human Nature* he famously writes:

In every system of morality, which I have hitherto met with, I have always remark'd, that the author proceeds for some time in the ordinary way of reasoning, and establishes the being of God, or makes observations concerning human affairs; when of a sudden I am surpriz'd to find, that instead of the usual copulations of propositions, *is*, and *is not*, I meet with no proposition that is not connected with an *ought*, or an *ought not*. This change is imperceptible; but is, however, of the last consequence. For as this *ought*, or *ought not*, expresses some new relation or affirmation, 'tis necessary that it shou'd be observ'd and explain'd; and at the same time that a reason should be given, for what seems altogether inconceivable, how this new relation can be a deduction from others, which are entirely different from it.[2]

'You cannot derive an *ought* from an *is*'. After Hume, this doctrine attained almost the status of a dogma in Western European thinking.[3] It has, however, been questioned in recent times. And it is, indeed, highly questionable. The thing looks, in the first place, not quite so obvious if instead of talking about what *ought* to be, we talk about

---

2 A *Treatise of Human Nature*, Book III, Part I, Section 1. I quote from p. 469 of David Hume, *A Treatise of Human Nature*, ed. L. A. Selby-Bigge, 2nd edn revised by P. H. Nidditch (Clarendon Press, Oxford, 1978).

3 In a famous paper, 'Hume on "Is" and "Ought"' (*The Philosophical Review* LXVIII (1959)), Alasdair MacIntyre argues that, in the text I have just quoted, Hume is not, in fact, propagating an is/ought dichotomy but merely attacking one particular way (by an appeal to belief in God) of deriving what ought to be from what is. Hume does

cont.

what is *good* or *bad*. For the kind of ethical thinking that I shall be trying to expound, doing what you *ought* is just one particular kind of morally good behaviour. It is behaviour that is sanctioned by just law, and obedience to such law is good because it is necessary for living in society, and living in society is part of the good life. So for this way of thinking *ought* is a secondary and derivative idea.

Let us, then, formulate the problem thus: Can we say that something is *good* because of what we know that it *is*?

People who follow Hume think that while you can, in principle, give a complete account of what a piece of human behaviour *is* in objective terms, upon which all observers can agree, you cannot derive from this the proposition that the behaviour is morally good or bad, that this is a subjective matter for each observer.

But this doctrine looks, in fact, pretty strange. For in every ordinary use of 'good' and 'bad', saying that something is *good* because of what it *is*, is *exactly* what we do. According to Humean thinkers, there is one tone of voice in which we say exactly what is being done, what a piece of human activity is, and quite another in which we praise it or say it is good or bad. But the truth seems to be that this separation of values from facts is ordinarily thought of as the mark of someone who is not very good at mak-

3. *cont.*

    this, says MacIntyre, in order to prepare the way for his own more 'Aristotelian' appeal to human passions and desires. It seems to me, however, that, on the face of it, there is a difference between Hume's appeal to our empirically 'observed' passions and the Aristotelian appeal to human needs, interests, desires, and happiness. MacIntyre himself stresses this in later writings. Cf. *After Virtue* (Duckworth, London, 1981), especially Chapter 16.

ing value judgements, someone who is not a reliable guide to what is good or bad.

I once switched on the television and recognized, with a shudder, that it was showing yet another programme devoted to ice-skating. I was just about to change channels when I saw two people doing the most amazingly beautiful things. I was an instant convert to ice-skating, or, at least, to watching it, and I subsequently discovered they were people that everyone else had known about for months. I watched them avidly and incessantly. One day I was watching them and saying things like 'Beautiful', 'Lovely', 'Marvellous' – all expressions of value. With me was a friend who was equally enthusiastic but also knew something about ice-skating. He expressed his enthusiasm by saying things like 'Say, look at the way she did that ...', and there followed a stream of arcane jargon. The air became thick with talk about double salchows, the toeless lutz, reverse walley jumps, and the double cherry flip – all of which expressions were describing scientifically, and I suppose accurately, what my skaters had just done, or, in some cases, not done. It was I, the ignorant amateur, who used what are supposed to be pure value expressions, whereas the person whose opinions and value judgements were worthy of respect (the one whom my skaters would have been pleased to hear) expressed his view that something was *good* precisely by describing what it *was*. In this case, the account of what it was, *was* an account, and the best account, of it being good.

But, of course, an objector may say: 'That is all very well for ice-skating, but we are talking about morals. It is one thing to say that X is a good ice-skater and quite another to say she is a good person.' And this, of course is true. But it would surely be very strange if the word 'good' in 'good skater' were used in some *totally* different way from its use in 'good person' – as though we were just making a pun with the word (a pun which, if it is such, is strangely made in many different languages). It would be very odd if 'good skater' could be spelt out in factual descriptions of what skaters do or can do (complex and open-ended descriptions, no doubt), whereas 'good person' were merely an expression of my feelings or desires.

I think people are forced into this very odd assertion because of a certain prejudice about persons. They are willing to agree that ice-skating is a particular definite art and activity – even though it is what I would call an open-ended activity. By calling it open-ended I mean that it is not just a technique which you either learn or do not learn. It is itself developing. What ice-skating henceforth involves will differ as new experts at it arise. Still, it is a definite human activity. These people I speak of, however, are unable to admit that human living, being a person, could be a definite human activity even in that open-ended sense. There may be many arts and skills within being human, but being human itself is not an art or skill. You may practise these arts well or badly, but you cannot practise being human itself well or badly. Now while I think, as I shall be saying, that there are important differences between those dispositions we call skills such as are constitutive of being a good skater, and those dispositions we call virtues, which are constitutive of a good person, nevertheless I think that being humanly good involves something very like skills.

The bone of contention here is this: To call people ice-skaters is to speak of them in terms of a role or function or a job they perform which they can therefore perform well or badly. But when we call people human beings, are we in any sense ascribing some role or function to them which they could perform well or badly?

The answer which I shall label 'individualist' says that we are certainly not. The human subject simply exists and that is that. The philosophers called 'existentialists' were, I think, asserting this with especial emphasis. Saying that 'existence is prior to essence', they seem to have meant that people first of all just *are*, and what categories they may fit into, what kind of being they are, what relationships they have with others, is a subsequent and secondary matter determined, in the case of 'authentic' people, by their own choices. Human beings may, for their own purposes, ascribe functions to things. I may make a spoon in order to eat my porridge, and it will be a good one if it fulfils the purpose I have given it, and a bad one if it does not. In a similar way, a group of people may invent the art and institution of ice-skating and similarly decide what makes for good skating and what for bad; all these purposes are ascribed by the decisions human beings make. We cannot, says the individualist, in the same way speak of human beings themselves as having been ascribed a purpose or role. Of course, human beings can be *given* roles, as when we appoint them as teachers or carpenters, and then they may be judged on objective grounds as good or bad teachers or carpenters. But we do not appoint people to be human beings, and so we cannot on any objective grounds say that they are good or bad human beings. For this individualist way of thinking, *purposes and roles are always human artifacts*: there are no purposes prior to human decisions; there are no purposes for human beings in themselves.

For this way of thinking, human societies are themselves simply human artifacts. There is no difference in principle between the *polis* and a club which a few congenial friends might decide to set up. I have called this way of thinking 'individualist' because it starts from the position that to be human is simply to be an individual; we are not equipped at birth with any role or function; we ascribe roles or adopt them by our own decisions. It is because people believe this to be self-evidently true that they are compelled to say that the phrase 'good man' must be used in a totally different way from 'good skater' or 'good spoon'. In the latter cases, 'good' can be spelt out objectively in terms of what is the case about the skater or spoon because their goodness is functional; in the case of 'good man', it cannot, because to be human is not to have a function.

Now, one way of replying to the individualist is to say: 'Ah, but it is not only human beings that ascribe purposes. God, too, can do this, and she has given human beings a purpose: we are thus objectively good or bad in so far as we fulfil these divine purposes in our lives.' Now this could mean one or other of two quite distinct things. It might mean that God has *happened to* give human beings a purpose as, if I have lost one of my chessmen, I might happen to use a button as a pawn. In that case God might easily not have had any purposes for human beings to be good or bad at, but he has in fact given them these roles to play, these jobs to do, these commands to obey. But if this is what is meant, my role as a piece in God's game is not in principle different from my role as a skater or teacher. I might not have had, but in fact do have, this role as, say, a teacher, and in virtue of that I can be a good or bad teacher. But just as the role given me by the Education Committee concerns my being a good *teacher* and not, as such, a good *person*, so the role given me by God would not concern my being a good person. God happens to have given me the job of, say, honouring my father and mother, and because of this I can be judged as a good or bad honourer of my father and mother, just as I might be judged a good or bad teacher. But in neither case would I be judged a good or bad human being. The penalties for being a bad honourer of my father and mother may be stiffer than the penalties for being a bad teacher, but that does not make any difference in principle. This kind of appeal to God as a role-ascriber does not, therefore, help us to find an actual role or purpose for the human being as such.

The other thing that might be meant by the appeal to God is not that God simply *happened* to equip human beings with a job or role but that in creating them as human beings God created things that intrinsically and necessarily, and of their nature, have roles or functions. God could no more have created a human being without function than she could have created a triangle without three sides.

Well that is fine: but in that case there is no need to bring God in at all (just as you do not have to bring in God to explain why triangles have three sides). If what you are claiming is that God just had to provide human beings with a role to be good or bad in, if what she created were to be human beings because *that is the kind of thing that a human being is* then you need to show that that *is* the

24

kind of thing that a human being is. And if you can do *that*, you already have a sufficient answer to the individualist without mentioning God at all.

So the appeal to God is either inadequate or unnecessary. If the individualist is to be answered, it can only be by trying to show that just to be human is, in fact, to have certain roles or functions – so that we can speak of people being good or bad at being human just as we can speak of them being good or bad at ice-skating. And this, I think, *can* be shown starting from the fact that to be human is to be political, to be part of a *polis*.

Let me retrace the thread of the argument: I want to show that just being human (not being human *plus* being, for example, a teacher or a mineworker, but just being human) involves having a role or job, such that we can not only say of people that they are good or bad teachers or mineworkers, but just good or bad *tout court*, good or bad people, in a way that can be spelt out by describing how they behave. Certain kinds of objectively describable behaviour would count as a reason for saying that someone is good or bad *tout court*, just as certain kinds of behaviour would count as a reason for saying that someone is a good or bad teacher or ice-skater. To say 'He can give an accurate though simplified account of the notion of surplus value, intelligible to an audience of non-economists, in twenty minutes' just *is* to say that, in this respect, he is a good teacher. I want to argue that to say 'He would give you the shirt off his back' just *is* to say that in this respect he is a good man. In other words, 'good man' is a descriptive expression just as 'good teacher' is. And I argue this because I argue that everybody is ineluctably political. The reason why being human entails

25

having certain functions to fulfil and roles to play (which may be done well or badly) is that to be human is to be part of a society of other human beings. To say 'This is a human being' is not like saying 'This is a red blob'. It is more like saying 'This is a gear-lever'. It would be hard to know what to make of the question 'Is this a good red blob?' But it is not at all hard to make sense of 'Is this a good gear-lever?'

Central to this argument is the claim that society is not the product of individual people. On the contrary, individual people are the product of society. There has to be at least some form of family society for people to be born at all and to survive and be brought up in a human way. And if you think of the family in the absolutely minimal terms of two parents producing a child, this structure itself depends on larger structures which ensure its survival and stability. The simplest social contract theory which supposes that individuals could come together initially for mutual support and protection to form a society is incoherent because it supposes these individuals to be already in possession of what only society could provide – institutions such as language, contract, agreement, and so on. The emergence of *homo sapiens* cannot have been (except maybe by a miracle) the evolution of strangely talented individuals. It must have been the evolution of new forms of animal grouping. We have to imagine the emergence of animal groups whose coherence is more and more a matter of conventional signs, language, rather than of innate signals. With this emergence of language, we begin to have rationality. Rationality is a special way of being in a group. It is because there is some form of linguistic community that there are rational individuals or 'persons'.

A linguistic community is a special sort of grouping in a very radical sense, for it changes the meaning of the word 'grouping'. The notions of whole and part are transformed. An individual person is, indeed, part of a society, but not simply in the sense that a gear-lever is part of a car. Individualism owes its popularity (despite its implausibility) to the sense people have that it must be wrong to treat persons as mere fragments or segments of a larger whole, as cogs or gear-levers. And this is understandable. There are, of course, totalitarian ways of thinking which are nothing but the obverse of individualism, which owe their popularity (despite their implausibility) to a craving people have to be treated as mere fragments of a larger whole, the craving to be rid of responsibility, to hand over decisions to the party, or the church, or the company, or the state. Both individualism and totalitarianism depend on the same mistake about the relationship of member and community in a symbol-using society. They see it as just like the relationship of part and whole in a pre-linguistic, non-rational group.

In the new kind of grouping, however, the linguistic community, what the part receives from the whole – language and rationality, the symbols in which she can represent herself to herself – are precisely what makes possible her specially human kind of individuality.

Let us contrast human individuals with cats. All cats are individuals, but this is because they are all born different and have had different things happening to them. But human beings are distinct from each other not just because of that. What they are like is the product not just of birth and what has happened to them but of their own rational decisions. Because we represent our *world* to ourselves symbolically, and because we can represent *ourselves* to ourselves symbolically, we can make free choices which determine our individuality. Our individual characters are importantly the product of our own decisions – though not, of course, only of our free decisions. It is just because of our insertion in the symbolic institutions of the linguistic society that we can, to a greater or lesser extent, make ourselves, possess ourselves and be free.

Moreover, we are free just to the extent that we are inserted in this human way into human community. It is the child who has been welcomed into the society of her family and friends, and encouraged to play a full part in it, who is able to be herself and be free. She has acquired the self-confidence and self-acceptance that comes of being accepted by others. And so it is at every level: it is by being parts that we are wholes. Community and individuality are not rivals. The individual who can stand over against the community, who can make a critical contribution to the tradition of the community, who can make a genuine contribution to revolution, is the product of that community and tradition. The individual, you might say, is the way in which a linguistic community develops itself historically. Other animal groupings do not have individuals in this sense. They do not have a *history*. They only evolve.

So it is through belonging to the community that you can make yourself the kind of person you are – so that you are not just passively made but actually make yourself, determine your life and character. In this way you make yourself the kind of person who can yet more make herself, whose life is more and more her own. This is, to speak generally, the role or task or function that belongs to being human. It is the task of entering more into the life of the community so that you can enter yet more; or, what is the same thing, it is forming your personality by your own decisions so that you have the personality which is more and more capable of making its own decisions. And this, still speaking generally, is what virtue is about. Virtues are dispositions to make choices which will make you better able to make choices. The aim of virtue is to be virtuous. Or, to go back to the other way of putting it, virtues are dispositions to enter into community, not to be absorbed in some lifeless way by a collective, but to develop those specifically symbolic, linguistic, rational relationships with others which we can sum up in the word 'friendship' and which are characteristic of the groupings of human animals.

This is, of course, to speak generally. There are many virtues and, while they all have as their long-term aim the community life of persons, they are each concerned with particular human activities. And a study of the virtues must be a study of the manifold ways in which people interact in the community of friendship.

If this is true (and I have only sketched it in the crudest way), there are many objections to be answered and qualifications to be made. But if it is true, then since to be a human being is to have the task of making yourself, the task of entering into the life of the community so that your life is more and more your own, then we have a basis for saying that, just as a good teacher is one who teaches well, so a good human being is one who enters into community well. The good human being is the one who is, in this sense, politically good. Aristotle's *Ethics* is simply the first part of his treatise on politics, on the life of the *polis*. If this is so, we ought to be able to describe what a good human being is in much the same way as we can describe what a good teacher is.

I am far from suggesting that you can easily describe what a good teacher is, or lay down simple rules for good teaching. It is fairly clear what a good typist is: he types accurately, neatly, and quickly, and that is it. Typing is simply a technique. It is not so easy to say what a good secretary is, for acting as a secretary involves many techniques. Being a teacher is more open-ended still, and being a human being immensely more so. There are clear rules for what counts as good typing. We cannot be anything like so clear about what counts as a good human being. Still we can say quite a lot. And that is what ethics is about.

What I have been saying has all been exceedingly abstract – far more abstract than, for example, Aristotle allows himself to be in his *Ethics*. There does not exist such a thing as a community in general any more than there is such a thing as a horse in general. There is, perhaps, not yet even a community in general in the sense of a single community of mankind of which particular communities are parts. There is certainly a single biological community, a 'family of man', a species in which we are all interfertile. But there is not yet a single political community. There are only particular geographical and historical communities, and to be a human being is to be born and brought up in one (or sometimes more) of these, with its own culture and tradition. A human being does not become herself by entering into community in general or into humankind, but by being educated into and responding creatively and critically to the tradition of her place and time.

The process of being educated in virtue is not one just of acquiring ideas. It is a matter of day to day living amongst particular structures and customs, as distinct from other structures and customs. It is in this sense a material business, a matter of this human body among others, even though the *way* of being among is not simply bodily in the sense that, say, a chip is among others in a computer, or even in the way that a wolf is among others in a pack. It is, as I have said, a matter of being among others through symbols and conventional signs. But these are still particular material symbols. Every language is a particular material language. The symbols of a society involve myths, manners, stories and language that belong especially to this people and not to others.

So even if we can show how we might make the phrase 'a good person' a descriptive expression in one culture, we have not yet shown how it might be universalized, how we might have a meaning for it which could be universalized, how it could be valid just for anybody of any culture who belonged to the human species. We face here the relationship of the biological and the historical/political, the two senses of human unity. And this is not just a theoretical but a practical problem. I suspect that we can speak of 'natural law' just to the extent that we have solved the practical political problem of bringing the biological and historical together, in so far as we have achieved 'one world', and not just one species.

Once we have taken account of the linguistic, the political, the historical (in order to make our case for seeing human beings as functional, role-playing beings), we have departed from the universality of the sheer biological species. Of course, membership of the biological species itself involves certain roles, especially sexual ones. But the natural life of a human being is immensely more complex than her sexual and species life alone. So although I can share my sexual *productivity* universally, being in principle interfertile with any member of the species of the opposite sex, when we come to cultural and moral creativity (and, thus, a transformed sexual creativity) – the activity by which I can create, not just the next generation, but myself and my own generation – we are in the realm of the local.

3

Politics and Virtue

I have been suggesting that to be a human being is to be a part of a larger whole. It is not just that human beings *join* groupings, as people join tennis clubs or political parties. There is a community to which we belong simply in virtue of being human. It is not one that we join, one that *we* constitute. It is a community that constitutes *us*. But what does this mean? In turning to this question I first want to compare and contrast our belonging to a community with the way in which other animals belong to a greater whole.

To be a dog is to be part of the species of dog. This is not merely a logical matter; it is not like saying that the dog belongs to the class of animals whose names in English begin with 'd' or to the class of four-footed beasts. When we say a dog belongs to a certain species we are referring to a distinct material entity, the race of dogs which has existed for a certain amount of time, has a certain evolutionary development and so on, and of which the dog is a physical part. There is no way of being a dog except by being born of members of this species. A very great deal of the important facts about a dog have to do with its derivation from this species – for example, a great deal of its behaviour can only be explained on this basis. An individual dog is the way the species is carried on (the way in which certain genes persist).

Now the same, of course, is true of the animal species *homo sapiens*. But in our case the thing becomes much more complex because what we belong to is not just a biological species. It is also some kind of linguistic community. And, while political or social communities constitute us rather in the way the biological species does, we also creatively respond to and modify them. Indeed, the linguistic community just *is* a community of such responsive and creative animals. In order to preserve itself in being, to be what it is, the linguistic community has to maximize the creativity of its members. If its members were determined by the community in the absolute way in which the individuals of a species are determined by their genetic structure, there would not *be* any linguistic community.

So there is a complexity or tension intrinsic to a linguistic community – at least by contrast with any mechanistic model of it. One cannot understand such a community successfully on the model of the parts going together to make a machine, or even on the model of the organs together forming an animal body (though that is a good deal nearer to the truth). It is characteristic of an animal that its parts are *organs* (tools, instruments). Their parts each have a life of their own which is simultaneously the life of the whole animal. The eye and brain of the dog have an operation quite distinct from the operation of the nose and brain. But both are the seeing and smelling of the animal as a whole. That is why what they do *counts* as seeing and smelling. Eyes cannot see; only the animal with eyes sees. This fact about an animal *is* the fact that it is alive; this is what Aquinas would refer to as its being animate, having an *anima* (soul).[1]

1 *De Spiritualibus Creaturis*, 11 and *De Anima*, 13.

Now this supplies us with a quite useful, even if inadequate, model for the linguistic community in which each member has an operation which is simultaneously the operation of the totality. This operation is the creation of *meanings*, which is the use of material things, like movements and sounds and marks, as *signs*. When I indulge in such creation I cease to be acting just as me, just as *this* individual. I enter into the language. That is why my statements, for example, are not just bits of *my* biography but have an objectivity, which transcends me. This is connected with the interesting fact that in the sentence, 'I think that p' (where p stands for any proposition you like), the clause 'I think that ...' can always be dropped without loss (except in the special usage in which 'I think' means 'I'm not sure', or in the usage according to which you are supposed to take note, not of what I think, but of the fact that *I* think it). 'I think that p' is not, in general, a statement about *me* at all. Its role is just to assert that p is the case.

This means that in creating meanings, in using language, I behave in a way that is not simply individual. Aquinas makes the same point when he says that the act of understanding is not a corporeal act, when he says that, when understanding, I transcend my materiality, which for him is my individuality.[2] Matter for him is the principle of individuation, of privacy. Averroes (Ibn Rushd, 1126–1198) took this point very seriously. He maintained that there is no such thing as an individual mind. There is but one mind (as we might say, the language, the *discourse*) and we individually latch onto that. For Averroes, what is particular to each of us is not strictly our understanding, which is

2 *Summa Theologiae*, 1a, 79.

universal, but the images we form when we think, which are material. Aquinas wrote one of the great Western philosophical classics, a little book called *De Unitate Intellectus contra Averroistas*, to argue that Averroes and his fans were going too far. In my thoughts, Aquinas agrees, I do indeed transcend my individuality. But, he says (and surely correctly) my thoughts are still *my* thoughts and no one else's. In some ways, Averroes resembled certain modern structuralists for whom (a) thoughts are in a language which speaks *through* the individual, and (b) literature is the product not of the private genius of the individual but of the culture or language itself. If Aquinas were writing today, I think he would, among other things, be engaged in literary theory, trying to steer a way between the older notion of the individual genius (with the 'author's intention') and the disappearance of the individual altogether in structuralism. For Aquinas, the spiritual is the *communal*. It is the immaterial, while materiality is individuality, privacy, subjectivity, isolation. So Aquinas speaks of even the animal senses as 'spiritual' because their operation is also an operation of the 'community', the whole animal to which they belong. This, of course, places Aquinas at the opposite pole from the Cartesian way of thinking according to which it is the spiritual that is private (a matter of my subjective consciousness) while it is the material, the body, that is public. For Descartes, we reach our real spiritual selves by withdrawing from the public material outside world into our own centres of consciousness. Not so for Aquinas.

It is true that Aquinas very frequently uses the metaphor of 'interior' versus 'exterior' when speaking of our spiritual or immaterial activities. It was a metaphor he inherited from Augustine. But he never speaks of subjectivity or *privacy*. My thoughts really are *my* thoughts, he insisted against Averroes. But they are not, and could not be, my *private* thoughts, except in the trivial sense that I do not always have to read or talk aloud. For Aquinas, I can use the common public language in which my thoughts are formulated to speak silently to myself as well as to speak to others. And, so Aquinas thinks, nobody need know what I think since I can keep a secret and tell lies. For him, however, that is not to say that thoughts are *essentially* private.

This very brief, and perhaps not very intelligible, excursus into Aquinas's theory of mind is intended to show how we are constituted as who we are not just biologically, by the species, but also culturally, spiritually, by the linguistic community, the *polis* in which we live. A *polis*, says Aristotle,

is something more than a pact of mutual protection or an agreement to exchange goods and services; for in that case [separate states like the] Etruscans and Carthaginians, and all others with contractual obligations to each other, would be taken as citizens of a single *polis*. Certainly, they have trade-agreements, no-aggression pacts, and written documents governing their alliance. But this is very different from being one *polis* with one citizenship ... neither is concerned with the *quality* of the citizens of the other, or even with their behaviour, whether it be honest or dishonest, except in dealings with members of the other *polis*. But all who are concerned with lawful behaviour must make it their business to have an eye

37

on the goodness or badness of the citizens. It thus becomes evident that that which is genuinely and not just nominally a *polis* must concern itself with virtue. Otherwise, the community (*koinonia*) is a mere alliance ... The *polis* is intended to enable all, in their households and their kinships, to live *well*, meaning by that a perfected and independent life.[3]

Aristotle is not, I think, suggesting that there might simply be an alliance or a non-aggression agreement *instead* of there being a *polis*. On the contrary, what he means by an alliance can only subsist between what are already constituted as states. What he is arguing against is an attempt to construe the *polis* itself as a very minimal kind of relationship, like an international agreement or a trade-post – the attempt, in fact, of modern neo-conservatism. He goes on: 'There arise in the *polis* the family connections, brotherhood, common sacrifices, games which draw men together. But these are created by friendship, for the will to live together is friendship. The end of the *polis* is the good life and these are the means towards it.'[4]

So to summarize: the *polis* is that because of which there are linguistic animals at all, and the purpose of the *polis* is that these animals should flourish, should live the life becoming to them, which is simply to live fully in the *polis*. In this sense, by existing so that its members may lead the good life, the *polis* exists *for its own sake*. For Aristotle, politics is the study of how to maintain the *polis* and the first part of that study is ethics. This is the back-

3 Aristotle, *Politics* III, 9.
4 Ibid.

ground to Aquinas's treatment of virtues. He says: 'Since man by his nature is a political animal, moral virtues, insofar as they are natural to him, are called political virtues, for on them depends his behaving well in social life.'[5] This interesting text is not, indeed, central to Aquinas's treatment of virtues. In it he is simply explaining the term 'political virtues' (an expression in use in his time). But it illustrates very well the Aristotelian assumptions in his thinking.

The *polis*, then, needs that people should be virtuous. It is also the means by which people become virtuous and grow in virtue. This is what the *polis* is for, so we are here speaking of the healthy *polis*, the one that fulfils its function, one that really grows as a *polis*. This, of course, provides us with a critical standard by which we may judge any particular historical society. To what extent does it foster the virtues of its citizens? Aristotle laments the state of Athens 'nowadays' by comparison with 'the old days': 'Formerly, as is natural, every one would take his turn of service [sc. in political office]; and then again, somebody else would look after his interest, just as he, while in office, had looked after theirs. But nowadays, for the sake of the advantage which is to be gained from the public revenues and from office, men want to be always in office.'[6]

Well, of course, we are all a bit like that. So any actual society is not only the source of virtue for its citizens but also corrupt and the target of the virtuous person's criticism and challenge.

But even the most corrupt society with a ruling class bent almost exclusively on its own private material advantage

5 *Summa Theologiae*, Ia2ae, 61, 5. My translation.
6 Aristotle, *Politics*, III, 6.

requires that its citizens should be inclined to act justly. It is not simply that it requires that people should do the things that justice demands, like telling the truth and not defrauding each other (for people might do these things out of fear of punishment or for some other reason); it is necessary that people should themselves be *inclined* to act in this way, be disposed to act in this way, and this is for them to have acquired the virtue of justice. People who are disposed in this way, people who love justice, are, of course, very liable to become a threat to the ruling class of a corrupt society. But this is just one of the contradictions inherent in the unjust society – it cannot afford to guard against the threat by getting rid of justice altogether. That would be to descend from free enterprise and competition into sheer chaos.

One who has the virtue of justice, then, is one who has learnt to want the things that are just. It is not that he acts justly because he wants to *have* something else, like honour, or to *avoid* something, like prison. Honesty may well be, in the end, the best policy, and that, perhaps, is why it is a virtue at all. But, as Archbishop Whateley of Dublin (1787–1863) says in the *Oxford Dictionary of Quotations*: 'Honesty is the best policy; but he who is governed by that maxim is not an honest man.' A child learns to read initially because she wants to please her parents or teachers, so the reading is seen as good because it has good ulterior consequences. This shows itself in the fact that if those same consequences can be achieved in some other, and perhaps easier, way (say, by pretending to read a passage that is known off by heart), the child may well prefer to do this. Similarly, the man who does the just thing for the sake of praise and honour might do an unjust thing if the same reward were available for it. But in consequence of continued reading at her parents' behest, the child in most cases discovers that books are delightful in themselves and that reading is a good and pleasant way of spending time. She enters whole new worlds of imagination and so on. She is now reading for its own sake and now there is no longer any point in ever pretending to read. It is the good *intrinsic* to reading that she seeks, no longer an ulterior consequence. Now education involves a similar process with regard to acting justly. We begin by acting well because we want to please our parents or others. We end by wanting to be the kind of person who is just and not cowardly and so on, just as the child wants to be a reading person: in both cases, it is a matter no longer of pleasing the grown-ups but wanting to *be* grown-up.

The just person is one to whom the just thing appeals. We may contrast that with the law-abiding person. True, the just person will in many (perhaps most) cases be law abiding, but there is a difference. By 'the law-abiding person' I mean one who acts in a certain way precisely because the law commands it. Her formal object, you might say, is the law itself. It is the keeping of the law that matters to her, not precisely the nature of the action done. Such a person, then, will do *whatever* the law commands; and what counts as a command of the law is to be determined by discovering who is the legitimate authority and what this authority has in fact decreed. In this sense, the law-abiding person applies an *external* criterion to the action. I mean that when you have described the action in human terms, it is an *additional*, external fact that it is commanded or prescribed by some authority. The just person, however, who acts because she loves justice, or out of justice, is not applying an *external* criterion. For to be just is to want, to be disposed, to do things that are just. And whether something is just, unlike whether it is commanded, depends simply on the nature of the action itself. A disposition is internally related to its object. The disposition of justice is simply the disposition to do just things and to refrain from unjust things. So the virtue has to be defined by beginning with the nature of the things that are just, and this we will be looking into in a moment.

First, though, there are two questions I should like to open for discussion. The first is this: I mentioned earlier that in the statement 'I think that p' the first three words are in some way both misleading and redundant. They make it look as though the statement were a proposition about me, as though 'I' were the name of the subject being talked about. In fact, this is not so, as is shown by the redundancy of the apparent reference to me. This, I suggested, is connected with the speaker's capacity to transcend her individuality and materiality. Now it seems to me that 'I want to do X' is a rather similar case. It looks on the face of it like a piece of autobiography just as 'I think that p' looks like a piece of autobiography. But in neither case are we dealing with a statement about a subject (me) that is named by the first word of the sentence, 'I'. In 'I want to do X', the first two words are almost as redundant as the first three words in 'I think that p'. If you shave them off, you get simply 'to do X'. Now that, of course, unlike 'p', is not a sentence, at least not an ordinary one, but a clause, and so the cases are not exactly the same. Nevertheless, there are even English usages in which 'to do X' would be a sentence. Hamlet says: 'To sleep: perchance to dream: ay, there's the rub ...' Now, here 'To sleep' is not just the name of an action or whatever. It expresses a wanting to sleep (the sleep of death) which is then checked by the thought of the dreams. There is in any case no difficulty at all in imagining a language in which desires would always be expressed simply by sentences like 'O, to be in England', or 'O, to get my hands round his throat'. This would have the advantage that such expressions would not be likely to be confused with autobiographical remarks about the speaker. The speaker both in 'I want to do X' and in 'O, to do X' is saying the same thing. She is indicating that doing X is concretely (not just in a general way) *desirable*. She is not talking about herself. Just as the speaker in 'I think that p' is indicating that p is *true*, she is not talking about herself.

I mean to suggest that 'I want to do X' differs in an important way from 'I would get a kick out of doing X', which *does* seem to talk about me, to add a piece of autobiography. Of course, '*I* think that p' differs a great deal from '*She* thinks that p', which is a piece of biography and in which the first three words are by no means redundant. Similarly, '*She* wants to do X' is a piece of biography. But 'I want to do X' does not itself say anything about me; it expresses a desire to do X, or, what is the same thing, expresses the concrete desirability of doing X. 'I want to do X' no more announces the discovery of the fact that I have a desire in me, than 'I think that p' announces the discovery that I have a thought in me.

The second thing I want to notice before going on to asking what just actions are is that the virtue of justice raises what we might call the 'Thrasymachus question' in its purest form.[7] Let me explain.

Suppose we establish that people need society; and suppose we establish that society needs people to be just. Does it follow that people need to be just?

Thrasymachus – but, for the sake of brevity, let us henceforth call him Fred instead – certainly needs society. He needed it in order to be born, to learn to speak, and to receive all the education, all the skills, that he has. And this society could not have existed without there being a preponderance of people who acted justly most of the time. And this could not have been achieved unless most of them possessed to some degree the virtue of justice. You could not have a literate society unless most people got beyond the stage of reading to please others and arrived at the state of reading for their own enjoyment. Similarly, you could not, I think, have a society in which people acted justly unless most of them had got beyond the state of simply doing it out of desire for rewards or fear of punishments.

Fine: but is there any reason that Fred could have why *he* should be just? Fred, we may suppose, is perfectly prepared to act justly when it is rewarded, but equally prepared to act unjustly when that brings *its* rewards. This means, by our account of the matter, that he is not a just man. Now why should he be (so long as other people are)?

I do not think that it is a valid answer to say that, as a matter of fact, in the long run justice always will be

---

7 Thrasymachus of Chalcedon was a Greek sophist active during the last three decades of the fifth century BC. He appears as a character in Plato's *Republic* where he raises the question 'Does it pay to be just?'.

rewarded and injustice punished by the all-seeing God. This is not because Fred may doubt the existence of such a celestial police-force and tribunal, but because to do just acts simply from calculation of celestial rewards and punishments is not to act justly. Christians, for example, hold that to do just acts simply and solely to avoid going to hell will not prevent you from going to hell. What will prevent you from going to hell is charity, and that is quite different.

I would try to answer this question (Why should Fred be just?) by first noting that I address my answer to Fred. I am trying to give *him* a reason for being just. A great deal now hangs on what *for him* would count as a reason for doing anything. Now being just is *itself* having certain kinds of reasons for doing things or not doing them. A just man will see it as a good reason for not making a confession under threat of torture that it would be cowardly. To have a virtue *is* to count certain considerations as reasons for acting.

Perhaps it is the case, then, that Fred who asks 'Why should I be just?' is simply an unjust man asking *his* typical questions: What's in this for me? What is the external reward or punishment involved in doing this or being like that? Now these are exactly the questions I might imagine a child asking before she can read. (Of course, being a child, she would be unlikely to ask them, but she would behave as one who had asked and answered them by saying: 'In order to please these grown-ups, or at least not to offend them.')

This fact about the child does not throw us into philosophical perplexity. We simply set about teaching her. She will find out for herself reasons for thinking it intrinsically good to be able to read (to acquire and develop the disposition or skill of reading). And what is true of the literate child is also true of the non-just child. She too discovers in doing just acts that their desirability does not lie simply in, as she first supposed, pleasing the grown-ups. She finds them intrinsically desirable. Now perhaps the difference between Fred and the child lies in nothing more than that he asks the question explicitly in a way that the child would be unlikely to. If so, the proper response is not to seek to answer this question in his terms, but to do for Fred what we do for the child – persuade him to do what is in fact just in the hope that he will begin to find justice desirable for its own sake.[8]

Now, there is a fairly obvious objection to all this. When the child or Fred grows up to value justice 'for its own sake' and not for love of rewards or fear of punishments, is he not simply *internalizing* these rewards and punishments? Have we not simply succeeded in creating in him a super-ego so that he is pleased with himself when he has pleased his internal monitor and feels guilt when he has displeased it? Whether the monitor is external or internal to Fred makes no difference to the real question, which is whether the good Fred sees in doing the just act is external or internal to that act. Someone who does just acts in order to be praised by his conscience is no more just than someone who does them to be praised by other people – that is, if you mean by 'conscience' a 'still small voice' or super-ego.

8 Aristotle says of very eccentric views ('opinions ... held by children and by the diseased and the mentally unbalanced'), 'The holders of such views are in need, not of arguments, but of maturity in which to change their opinions' (*Eudaimonian Ethics* I,3. I quote from J. L. Ackrill, ed., *A New Aristotle Reader*, Clarendon Press, Oxford, 1987, p. 481).

This objection is powerful because it does seem to describe accurately what often happens. We do often induce just such a super-ego or 'still small voice of conscience' which is no more than an internalizing of the pleasing-the-grown-up phase. But I would argue that in that case the educational process has failed. Supposing a child did indeed get beyond the phase of reading merely to please her teacher, but then merely passed into a phase in which she read because she felt guilty not to. (This is not an altogether imaginary case. Lots of people read Dostoievsky or Proust because they would feel guilty if they did not.) In such a case, the external teacher has simply been internalized, but the educational process has failed. It has failed because the child has not come to recognize the goods internal to reading. Can we not similarly say that the person with the super-ego or conscience has simply failed to see the goods internal to acting justly?

I think that if we are to make this comparison (between the skill of reading and the virtue of justice) stick, I need to say a little more about what happens when the child discovers the goods inherent to reading. It is not just that she experiences a new sensation which she happens to like. Someone who has hitherto only really liked sweet sherry might come to discover the pleasure of a light dry claret; someone whose chief indulgence has been in eating Turkish delight might be startled to find how delicious curry can be. In such cases, there is undoubtedly a progress because a new pleasant sensation has been found. But so far as that goes the progress might have been the other way round, from claret to sweet sherry, from curry to Turkish delight. In either case, it would have been a simple addition to the catalogue of nice tastes.

Now discovering the goods inherent to reading is *not* like that. It involves something we might call an enlargement of the capacity for experience. The child finds a new way of being in the world. The world is no longer restricted to what she and her immediate circle experience. She can share the experience and imagination of vast numbers of others. She has, most importantly, discovered a new activity, a new way of being *active*, which is very different from discovering a new sensation, a new way of being *passive*. In fact, learning to enjoy story-books and other books is part of growing up. It is the kind of thing that (except for special accidental circumstances) *no one could ever regret*. To have discovered the goods inherent to reading is to have become in one respect a more fulfilled, a more excellent person with many more possibilities and opportunities open to one.

Now when I want Fred to become just, it is this sort of thing I want for him. The problem is merely to get *him* to want it for himself. I think that the only way to do this is to discover the complex things that he does want (which will turn out to be by no means simply pleasing sensations), and to indicate how the practice of just acts is involved in these activities and how the disposition to act fairly is needed for them, so that he begins to recognize his own desirable activity as involving justice together with other virtues and thus begins, perhaps slowly, to see that justice is desirable. It is not just an argument or just a way of acting, a regime that we are prescribing for Fred, but an 'argumentative regime', a matter of reasoned practice or of the practical reason. I will convince Fred that he has reason to be just, not merely by talking (theoretical or 'speculative' reason) nor by brainwashing, simply bullying him into doing just actions for so long that he begins to bully himself (the development of a super-ego or conscience), but by persuading him to engage in reasoned activity, activity in which he is analysing what he is doing and why: exercising him in the question, given the facts, 'What is it reasonable to do?' In fact, Fred and I would be engaged in what Aristotle or Aquinas would recognize as Ethics – a study which is not simply about how to *talk* about being good but is intended to *make* people good as well. For Aristotle, ethics was part of politics. In our own day, very little that he would see as ethics is taught in the philosophy departments of universities (or at least not until very recently). The people he would recognize as doing ethics today would be people engaged in a certain kind of political thinking. Aristotle would most certainly have deep disagreements with Marxist thinkers, but when he heard them say 'Philosophers have sought to explain the world, the point is to change it', he would recognize them as at least on his wavelength. However wrong they may be, what they are wrong about *is* ethics.

So part of our task with Thrasymachus or Fred is to show him that acting justly is involved in things he wants to do and engage in. A preliminary to this is getting rid of his illusion that what he wants is not to engage in activities and do things, but simply passively to receive experiences. It is, or at least it used to be, quite a common belief among philosophers that a man might hold that the only reason for doing anything is to get an experience (a pleasant, satisfying experience) as a result. The logic of this view is that if you could get the experience some other more convenient way you would not bother with the activity. Aquinas in discussing what he calls *beatitudo*, blessedness, the end

of human activity, begins by asking if it could be constituted by what amount to various kinds of experience. He
ends by arguing that it has to be itself an activity.
Fundamentally, his reason for thinking this is that it is in
its proper activity that a thing reaches its perfection. It
exists, so to say, at full stretch; it is itself most fully.[9]

One convenient modern device for making the same
point is Robert Nozick's 'Experience Machine'.[10] You have
to imagine some kind of tank in which you can float and
in which you can be plugged in to electronic devices
which stimulate your brain to receive any experience you
choose, in any variety you choose. The only stipulation is
that you will have to be in the machine for the rest of your
life.

The first part of the 'thought experiment' is to ask
whether you yourself would choose to be plugged into any
series of pleasurable bodily sensations as you lay in the
tank. To answer 'No' to this is to see the point of Aquinas's
rejection of such pleasure as equivalent to blessedness.

But the machine is more versatile than that: it can go
through the successive articles of *Summa Theologiae*
1a2ae, 2 giving you experiences of being rich, honoured
and famous. And, finally, it can give you the sensation and
pleasure of activity. It can simulate for you all the experience you would have in winning the London and New
York Marathons, or discovering the cure for cancer, or
writing a play as great as *King Lear*. Now how about that?
Would you choose a lifetime in which you have these
experiences while as a matter of fact you are doing none

9 See Aquinas, *Summa Theologiae*, 1a2ae, 3, 2.
10 Robert Nozick, *Anarchy, State and Utopia*, (Oxford University Press,
 Oxford, 1974) pp. 42–45.

of these things but simply floating in a tank in a laboratory? The question is: Would you now choose to be so plugged in? – not, would you enjoy yourself once plugged in? Once plugged in you would in fact be unable to want your situation changed. So this too depends on your decision now.

To discover that you would not want this illusion, however satisfying, is to discover that it is not the *satisfying* but the *satisfactory* life that we really want. By 'satisfactory', I mean (etymologically) the sufficiently (*satis*) made (*factum*) life, the life which in actual *fact* is fulfilled. It is to see the point of Aristotle's remark that no people would choose to live with the intellect of a child throughout their lives, however much they were pleased by the things that please children.[11] The experience machine could give you the experience of writing a great novel, or overcoming danger, or being a wonderful surgeon. But, in fact, you would have done nothing, and when your brain finally rots it could be said of you that you never really lived.

Now, if Fred will come along with us thus far – if he recognizes that his happiness lies not in experiences themselves but in certain kinds of activities – then it may be possible to show him the worth of justice and other virtues by showing how they are implied in such activities.

There is a very large number of, perhaps an indefinite number of, complex fairly large-scale activities which people find worthwhile and wish to engage in. Plainly, I am not going to even try to deal with them all or to find any general principles upon which we could deal with them in

11 See Aristotle, *Eudemian Ethics*, 1, 5 (1215b).

bulk. What we need to do is to look at each such activity as it occurs to us and see how in fact it is carried on.

I am going to instance making and maintaining a family. I am concerned here with what Peter Geach calls 'large-scale worthy enterprises' and Alasdair MacIntyre calls 'practices'. These are all parts of what Aquinas calls political or social life. Aquinas sets this within the context of what he calls *the* end of man, blessedness (*beatitudo*), and he seeks to show that the political virtues, the cardinal virtues, take their place in the deepest meaning of human life, which is our vocation to the heavenly *polis*, the divine life. Philosophers of the kind that we might call neo-Aristotelians often agree in rejecting Aquinas's argument to show that there is one last end for mankind. They accuse him of the familiar logical slip of moving from 'every human activity has some end' to 'there is some end that every human activity has' (i.e. some one end). I am inclined to think they are right about this – though of course the fact that Aquinas produces a bad argument for some doctrine does not make that doctrine false. I would like to argue that the place for considering the unit of mankind's purpose, the single last end common to all people of all cultures is at the *end* of the study of ethics, rather than the beginning. I agree with Geach that there are sufficient grounds for seeing the virtues as goods and for understanding, at least in part, their significance if we simply look at the 'large-scale worthwhile activities' in which people do in fact want to engage.[12] When we have done that, if we discover a necessity for the virtues, then we can widen our sights to the whole political community

12 P. T. Geach, *The Virtues* (Cambridge University Press, Cambridge, 1977), Chapter 1.

(politics as the greatest large-scale worthwhile activity), and from there to what we might call the politics of mankind. And it is here that we will see coming towards us the politics of the Bible, meeting us from, so to say, the other direction.

But for the moment let us just consider the various large-scale activities; I mean large scale by contrast with, say, knitting or bricklaying. Here is MacIntyre's attempt to give an account of what he calls a 'practice' in one large-scale complex worthwhile sentence. Remember when reading it that he has in mind some such activity as 'the making and sustaining of family life'.

> By 'practice' I am going to mean any coherent and complex form of socially established cooperative human activity through which goods internal to that activity are realized in the course of trying to achieve those standards of excellence which are appropriate to, and partially definitive of, that form of activity, with the result that human powers to achieve excellence, and human conceptions of the ends and goods involved, are systematically extended.[13]

Let us look at that as an account of making and maintaining a family life, which is quite likely to be one of the activities that Fred may want to engage in.

Having and maintaining a family as an activity of parents is complex, coherent (in the sense that it is a distinguishable form of activity with its own pattern to it), and, of course, cooperative – and here the cooperation is a matter not only of relations between the two parents and

13 Alasdair MacIntyre, *After Virtue* (Duckworth, London, 1981), p. 175.

their children but also many other agents and agencies essential to family life, like grocers, schools, and so on.

In maintaining a family we are concerned with goods internal to activity. That is: we do not maintain a family in order to realize some good which might have been attained some other way. In this sense, running a family is 'for its own sake'. These goods are achieved in the course of trying to achieve certain standards of excellence that belong to running families (making sure that the children are healthy, adequately fed and clothed, educated, and so on, that the family forms a coherent unity in friendship, that it plays its part as a family in appropriate social activities, hospitality and all the rest) with the result that human powers to achieve these excellences are systematically extended, so that not only do these parents get better at the job but throughout a section of history the activity of maintaining a family becomes better understood and practised. And finally throughout such a personal life and such a history the idea of what a family *is*, and what the goods are that belong to it are gradually revised and extended. To put it simply, by trying in practice to be good parents we deepen our notion of what it is to be a parent.

You may well feel that in these last respects the family is not a particularly good example to take. It is highly debatable whether the modern family is a great improvement on families of the past – though hardly debatable that it is an improvement on some, especially in the more recent past. But this is where it matters that all our practices are interlocking and the family is radically affected by changes in the economy and in society in general. MacIntyre's own preferred examples of practices are such things as the practice of physics or portrait-painting or architecture.

Now if you think of what is involved in engaging in such a practice as running a family it becomes clear fairly soon that it cannot be done unless it is possible to rely on the justice of others and unless others can rely on your inclination to act justly. Without this there could not be the stability over time and over varying circumstances that is essential to rearing a family. Faithfulness to vows, regard for the rights of husbands and children and wives is plainly required – and it is not simply that people will act in accordance with just demands but that they should cultivate the disposition to act in this way, which comes from continually so acting; in other words, the virtue of justice.

Again, a family will tend to fall apart if the people involved are simply at the mercy of their passions. If they let their anger rip or else repress it only with an effort of will so that it goes underground, if they act upon every passing sexual attraction, or again merely repress this with an effort of will, if, in fact, they lack the virtue of temperance, the project of a family is doomed. And such virtues are acquired precisely in this kind of context. Courage is required in adversity, and the patience that goes with courage. And, of course, above all there is required the moral/intellectual virtue of good-sense, knowing what to do in order to realize the goods of family life in these particular circumstances. These human qualities or dispositions are distinguishable from the skills that are also associated with maintaining a family, like being able to cook; and one important distinguishing feature is that these qualities or virtues turn out to be required in other important fields of activity. Maintaining a university department, for example, does not, except very marginally, involve being able to cook, but it does demand just those human qualities that are needed in the first case. We are dealing here, then, with dispositions which are necessary for a particular worthwhile venture or practice but are not confined to or defined by that practice. There are skills required for a good ice-skater which simply constitute her as a good skater; but she will also require certain virtues in order to become and remain a good skater which go beyond skating, and it becomes possible to speak of the dispositions proper to a human being as such or at least the dispositions belonging to any human being in this culture, in this historical epoch. I am not of course suggesting that because so and so is a great skater, she is for that reason a great and outstandingly good human being; I am suggesting that without some of the human qualities that we would praise in any human being we come across, it would not be possible to be a great skater. She may well counterbalance this with terrible human failings. But some of the virtues need to be there.

But this raises the question of the unity of the virtues. Can you have a genuine virtue while being otherwise quite vicious? Aquinas held that you could not. A thoroughly unjust man could not be truly courageous. He could only have a semblance of courage.[14] In the end, Aquinas held that no virtue is authentic unless it is, as he puts it, informed or enlivened by charity.[15] Others have disagreed with this. For the moment we might at least say that you can have some virtues more intensely, and others quite feebly.

14 See *Summa Theologiae*, 2a2e, 123.
15 See *Summa Contra Gentiles*, 4, 55.

This, then, is how I would deal with Fred (Thrasy-machus). I would try to show that there are human virtues which are necessary to practices in which he wishes to engage, in which he will find some part of his happiness. The deliberate cultivation of these virtues is thus seen to be necessary to a happy adult active life. Certain of these virtues, such as courage and justice, will dispose him to act in ways that may bring disaster to him, he may be cruci-fied. This is a risk that he needs to face if he is to engage in such adult life; and, of course, courage is itself the virtue that will enable him to take such a risk. The alter-native, however, is to live the half-life of the man floating in the tank, to opt for not growing up because growing up may involve unpleasantness. To someone who says that he does opt for such a passive life of immaturity there is, I think, nothing to be said.

I do not, by the way, think that it can be shown to any-one that being virtuous is always going to be in his inter-ests, always going to ward off disaster. I do not think it will do to say that human beings need virtues even if it kills them, to say, as Geach puts it, that 'an individual bee may perish by stinging, all the same bees need stings'.[16] This response is not good enough because it is not an argument directed at an individual bee who is asking pre-cisely whether to use its sting or not. The analogy does not work because it is always fatal to the bee to use its sting. Justice and courage, however, are not always fatal and perhaps will never be in a particular life. Whether they will be fatal is a matter of chance. What is certain is that they are necessary to adult happiness.

16 Geach, *The Virtues*, p.17.

4

Organism, Language and Grace

This chapter, which picks up on, and to some extent elaborates on, what I have said above, is meant to be an agenda, or, more pedantically, a *cogitanda* for thinking about what it means to be alive. It will be divided into three parts: first, about being alive instead of inanimate or mechanical; second, about being humanly alive instead of being a brute animal – to have a life-source; and third, about being divinely alive – to have eternal life. So I will be talking in turn about organism, language and grace, and I shall be seeing them as a development and expansion of the notion of meaning itself, and its connection with story. One of my first propositions will be that to be alive is to exist in a world of meanings. There is the meaning that belongs to organic structure, the meaning that belongs to a life-story, an enacted narrative, and the meaning that belongs to having the life-story of God.

There is a not-very-hidden agenda as well. I see this chapter as a skirmish in the war between Aristotle and Descartes. I see this war as a liberation struggle to free us from the shackles of Cartesian dualism, the mind/body dualism that permeates our culture and our society. (And this is not just a metaphor: I see this skirmish as a tiny contribution to the liberation of our world from bourgeois presuppositions that have quite definite oppressive economic and political correlatives. A restatement of Aristotle is always a subversion of certain notable politicians.)

One difficulty we have to face in conducting the skirmish is that it is no longer possible to re-state Aristotle in his own terms. Practically all of these have been co-opted by the enemy and turned to Cartesian uses. So this chapter is an agenda for thinking in an Aristotelian and materialist way without being cluttered with a poisoned vocabulary.

To be alive, said Aquinas (one of Aristotle's most perceptive commentators) is to have a principle of movement from within, to be *automobile* – taking movement in a fairly broad sense for any kind of activity. Life is some kind of autonomy, some kind of independence or freedom, some kind of self-originating. Fred is alive when, if one part of Fred moves another part of Fred, Fred is moving Fred. This occurs just when each *part* of Fred *is* Fred. This is the case when the parts of Fred are organs or are *organisms*. An organ is a part of a structure which is most fundamentally defined as a part of the whole structure. It is a part whose whole being is to be functional. So the legs and eyes and claws of a jaguar exist as functioning parts of the jaguar – they do not first exist in their own right; they first exist as parts of the whole. So if you are so ill-advised as to pat the leg, you touch the whole jaguar; when you are then grasped by the claws, you are grasped by the whole jaguar. When the jaguar's brain moves its legs it is the whole jaguar moving the whole jaguar. This is what we mean by reckoning it to be alive. It is *self*-moving, automobile in this fundamental sense.

This will perhaps become clearer if we contrast this automobile jaguar with, say, a Jaguar automobile, an expensive car. The first car to arrive in a primitive community would quite naturally be thought of as alive. On the available evidence this would be a good guess. People would only revise their opinion and come to think, as we do, that it is not alive when they learn that the car is assembled from manufactured bits. The gears and wheels and tyres and windscreen wipers are even made in their different factories and brought together to make the assemblage we call the car. The car is made by organizing these already existing things according to a certain pattern so that they make contact with each other in certain interesting ways. The parts come first, and then there is a programme imposed on them.

The kind of thing we think of as living, however, begins as a genetic programme (inscribed, as we now know, in DNA molecules) and in virtue of this programme it grows the right cells to make up its various functioning parts. There are no parts you can assemble to make a horse or a jaguar; there is a primitive zygote or elemental horse or jaguar bearing the programme through which it develops its parts. You could say that the eye or the ear is first of all the jaguar and secondarily a particular chunk of stuff, whereas a wheel or a tyre is first of all this particular kind of thing and secondarily it is used as a part of a car. The point is a slightly slippery one to make because we usually *speak* of the bits of a car in the same functional way in which we speak of the organs of an animal, and this is simply because all machines are imitation animals. We talk of them metaphorically, as though they were animals. They are assemblages of bits that we have ingeniously put together to imitate in some ways the behaviour of animals. Since they usually only do the one thing that we want them to do, they do this one thing much more efficiently than animals. The oxen, besides pulling the plough, are preoccupied with the elaborate and time-consuming business of their sex-lives, of preserving and passing on the genes, the genetic programme without which no other oxen will be produced. We don't ask a tractor to reproduce itself and make other tractors; we can assemble them easily and cheaply in the factory. The tractor like any celibate can concentrate on the one job of work, pulling the plough or whatever.

Of course, if we wanted to, with computerization, we *could* program a very elaborate tractor to gather the necessary material and produce other tractors just like itself – with the same built-in program – and these would of course also reproduce themselves and so on. Then, since tractors were now no longer *assembled* but *reproduced themselves* according to their own genetic program, we would surely say that they were alive. We would have synthesized living tractors; but remember that the reason we would call them living is precisely that they would no longer be synthesized; they would have their independent, self-moving reproduction. The project, however, would be enormously expensive and tiresome and would run counter to the whole point of having machines in the first place – which is to be cheap *imitation* animals with just one or two functions that they do better than animals. So I don't recommend it. Having imitation animals is a good thing in itself; besides it is a first move in the liberation of real animals, just as having domestic animals, imitation slaves, was a first move in the liberation of real slaves. With animals, or any organisms, the whole, the genetic structure, is prior to the parts, unlike imitation animals, machines, in which the parts are prior to being assembled in a structural whole. This simple truth has very profound implications.

For with organisms we begin to have *meaning*. Let me explain.

The parts of an organism are essentially parts; I mean the first thing about them is that they are parts of the whole structure and it is secondary that they also have a character of their own. (They do not *exist* in virtue of having this character of their own but in virtue of the existence of the whole organism. This is what we perceive when we perceive the organism as alive as distinct from an inanimate structure.) There are, then, two levels of language at which we speak of any such organic part: we can talk of what happens in this individual bit of the structure or we can talk more fundamentally about how this is relevant to the whole structure. Thus we can talk about the rods and cones of the retina of the eye and the various photoelectric effects that occur in their organ; or we can talk of how these processes are relevant to the behaviour of the whole organism. In the first case we speak of the physiology of the eye and its nerves and so on; in the second case we speak of *seeing*. To talk of seeing or hearing or any other sensation is just to talk of the *relevance* of what goes on in some organ, some functional part, of the structure, to the behaviour of the whole structure. Sensation is not most obviously a matter of certain physiological changes in an animal but a matter of its behaviour. Thus the way to find out whether a particular animal can see or not is not to search for its eyes but to find out whether its behaviour is any different in the dark from in the light. To be able to see is to have your behavioural tendencies influenced by the illuminatedness of the world.

This whole way of seeing the matter is, of course, in strong contrast to the dualistic view which would see the physiological process of seeing or hearing as taking place in the *body*, while alongside it, the sensation itself is something that takes place in a *consciousness* or (in extreme cases) in a mind. The picture is of two processes, one causing the other, a process in the eye and a process in the consciousness. There is also a materialist version of the dualist picture which rather hopes that the brain will do for the consciousness. Things go on in the eye which result in the transmission of what are often called 'messages' through the optic nerves to the brain, as a result of which the brain sees. To say that the brain sees is as absurd as to say that my left ear is in love.

For the position that I have sketched, on the other hand, the connection and the distinction between the physiology and the sensation is not one of causal sequence but of logical level. To speak of sensations is to speak of physiology; but not the physiology of the eye in abstraction from its total context; to speak of sensation is to say what the optic physiology *counts as* for the whole organism. It is like the connection and the distinction between saying 'She waved her arm about in a particular way' and saying 'She greeted her friend across the street'. She was not doing two things. The greeting is not a separate event occurring in something called the consciousness of her and her friend; it is just the *meaning* of the physiological event of waving.

I said when I began that it has become impossible to re-state Aristotle in his own terms because his language has been co-opted to Cartesian use; and this discussion illustrates this. Aristotle expresses the truth that sensation is a physiological-process-in-its-relevance-to-the-whole-animal by saying that sensation is an operation of the psyche or soul, or form of the animal. But in consequence of the Cartesian victory over Aristotle the word 'soul' has been taken over to mean the Cartesian consciousness, a 'spirit' that is supposed to haunt the body, and so it is utterly misleading to use it anymore in an Aristotelian context. There were certain fundamentalist Cartesians who identified soul or consciousness with mind and so were constrained to say that brute animals cannot have sensations but are simply machines that provide an imitation of sensation. But for any Aristotelian, of course, it is as obvious and visible that other animals have sensations as it is that she has them herself.

The point of this rather brisk discussion of sensation is that it exhibits the connection between organic structure and meaning. Seeing or hearing is the *meaning* of what happens in the eyes or ears. Meaning is the relation of a part to the structure of which it is essentially a part. As we shall be seeing later, the meaning of a word is the part it plays in the whole structure of a language; to ask for the meaning of a word is always to ask about its relationship to other words; it is to ask for a definition. Just as seeing cannot be understood by looking at what goes on in the eye by itself, so linguistic meaning cannot be understood by looking at a word or phrase by itself. Sensations have to do with the complex behaviour of animals; meanings have to do with complex uses of language.

Eyes, optic nerves and sections of the brain are what the whole animal has sensations with. Similarly, words like 'yellow', 'perhaps', 'diagrammatic', 'hooray', 'although' and 'vouchsafe' are what the language has its meaningful uses with. As St Paul pointed out, the organs of the body are many and various; but they are nothing like as many and various as the bits of a language. But this is to anticipate.

Meaning has a functional place in a complex structure. The sense organs of an animal are the means by which its world is meaningful to it. The forms and structures of the world around it are taken up into the complex organic structures of the animal body and thereby become meanings for that animal. When the jaguar takes in the scent and movement that characterize its prey it does not take the scents and movements as characterizing itself; it does not begin to smell or move like its prey; the immediate physiological effect on its nose or eyes is not what primarily matters. It takes in the scent and movements as meanings which will influence its behaviour. When the green light reflected from grass impinges on the hide of a white cow it makes it ever so slightly greener, but when it impinges on the cow's eye it becomes a significance, a meaning. It does not turn the eye green or if it does that isn't what matters; it turns the cow's munching in this or that direction. The greenness is received, as Aquinas would say, not 'naturally' but 'intentionally' as a factor in the cow's interpretation of and behaviour towards its world. What was simply a characteristic of the grass has become a meaning for the cow – and this is simply because the eye is an organic part of a complex structure.

Meanings are, if you like, second-order realities. A sensation (which is a meaning) is not what happens in an organ but the relevance of what happens in the organ to what is happening in other organs, and to the whole animal. Sensations are talked of at a higher logical level, in a second-order way, by comparison with talk of rods and cones and photoelectric discharges. With sensation, features of the world are raised to the level of meanings, the process of what Aquinas calls 'abstractio' has begun. But once again this is not language we can any longer use, for 'abstraction' has been co-opted by the empiricist wing of the Cartesian tradition to mean something quite other than 'raising natural features to significance' which is what it meant in the Aristotelian tradition. (For the empiricists, abstraction meant something like turning your attention to one feature and shutting your eyes to the rest.)

Just as the bits of an organism are essentially functional parts of an overall structure, so individual organisms can be seen as functional parts of a species. An animal species is not simply a logical class but a physical structure extending over time and space, beginning as a particular period in evolutionary history and spreading throughout some area of the world; a particular member of the species exists by being born of that species and its function can be seen as preserving and transmitting the genes that characterize the species. An individual cat is an organ by which the species of cat survives. It is this that accounts for so-called 'altruistic' behaviour on the part of individual animals – the mother sacrificing her life for her young and so on. It is because the individual animal is a functional part of the structure which is the species that certain aspects of the world have their meaning for it. Sheep do not have to learn that wolves are dangerous, grass edible, and rams sexually attractive; all these evaluations are necessary if there are to be any sheep for any length of time. Thus whether we are thinking of the nervous system of an animal or the system of the whole species, meaning is always the place of some aspect of the world 'raised up' to be within that system.

I have gone through all these platitudes simply because I want to compare and contrast the way in which human animals belong to a linguistic or cultural system with the way in which other animals belong to their physiological and genetic systems. It is characteristic of human animals to deploy symbols, to live in the structure we can broadly call language. What we call having a 'mind' is having the capacity to live in such structures, structures which, like the nervous system, or the genetic programme of an animal species, provide for meanings. Language is the nervous system of the human community. It is the context for meaning. The linguistic system of symbols is parallel to and comparable to the genetically provided system of meanings that govern the behaviour of all animals. Sheep and wolves are genetically provided with a system of meanings by which they interpret their world and in the case of many animals, perhaps most, this includes interpreting signals produced by other members of the species. So you get elaborate courtship rituals, signals of territoriality or aggression and submission – all that set of behaviours that are rather misleadingly called 'animal language'. It is misleading because although they are parallel, the radical difference between such signals and human language is that we *make our own* symbols. Of course like any other animals we inherit certain interpretations of the world and of the behaviour of our fellows, but the characteristic activity of the human animal is the creative development of language. This means that for us meaning is to be found not only in the structure of our bodies or in the programme of our genes but in structures we have our-selves created. We make meanings; we do not just find the world meaningful in certain ways. Nobody *inherits* the French language or even the Irish; instead of inheritance and evolution we have tradition and history. It is this cre-ative capacity to make new ways of interpreting the world that constitutes our freedom. In the new system of mean-ings there is included the possibility of the interpretation having been different; human language is the system of meanings that includes negation. When we choose to act in one way we might have chosen not to.

This perhaps will be a little clearer if we consider acting for a reason. Apart from the activities we call reflexes, ani-mal behaviour is not 'triggered' by the impact of the world on its senses. Animals are much too complex for that – it is the simplified imitation animals, machines, that are to be analysed in the simply Pavlovian way. In order to demonstrate an animal behaving as Pavlov decrees we have to restrict it artificially to one simplified form of behaviour. In fact, for any relatively complex animal its experience results not in an automatic response but in a tendency. The smell of a juicy bone may or may not make a dog salivate but it will give it a tendency to seek out the bone. This tendency, however, will be balanced and rela-tivized by a whole complex of other experiences. The ani-mal's behaviour is mediated by its total sensual evaluation of the world at any time, in other words, by meanings, by how it interprets its world. If it does go for the bone we will pick out certain of its tendencies as the reasons why it behaves in this way rather than that. We say the dog is running to the bone because it is hungry and it likes meat – I mean we talk this way when we are not being terrorized by theorists. A dog that has been trained in certain ways may very well *not* go for the meat, and in such a case we may judge that it avoids the meat unwillingly. We mean that there are reasons which would tend to make it go for the meat but these are overridden by other reasons such as its devotion to its master or fear or whatever. Animals, unlike simplified mechanisms, can act willingly or unwillingly and do so visibly. You can *see* a dog willingly and joyfully chasing a rabbit; you can *see* it slinking unwillingly back if it is called off. No building ever collapsed willingly or unwillingly; no computer ever reluctantly provided a printout. But we speak of animals being willing or unwilling precisely because their behaviour is mediated by knowledge, appreciation of meaning – in their case sensual meaning. But although brute animals can act willingly or unwillingly there is no possibility of their having acted differently. Their system of meanings does not include negation.

What is special about the human animals is that we not only, like the dog, have things we like to do and things we are reluctant to do, we also formulate aims and intentions for ourselves. This formulation or setting of aims can only be expressed by saying 'We did what amounted to saying to ourselves: "This is what I am trying to achieve and this is how I am going to achieve it"'. This is different from simply *having* an aim in that you might not have formulated it or set it for yourself. It is just this 'is-but-might-not-have-been' that language exists to express. Whenever I act intentionally it is always possible for you to ask me: 'What did you do that *for*?' Which is ordinarily to ask 'What story is that part of?' Whatever answer I give is informative precisely because there might have been other answers: 'This is the story and it might have continued differently.' In the case of the dog, the question 'What did it do that for?' is sufficiently answered by an accurate account of what it did in the context of the kind of beast that it is and the circumstances – if you get this answer right there are no other possibilities. While hunting, say, an animal may make very complex moves, taking one path rather than another, behaving with extreme cunning, but in the end what it does is the inevitable result of the various tendencies by which it is disposed. It is anthropomorphic to suppose that it is actually saying to itself: 'This will be the best way to do it.' We know this simply because the animal does not say to *us*, 'This is the best way to do it.' To suppose that there could be an invisible interior monologue without there being any exterior visible use of language is as foolish in the case of the leopard as it would be in ours. It is true in our case that we sometimes have thoughts we do not express, but this is only because we have thoughts we *do* express. Music consists partly of silences, but it could not consist entirely of silences.

For an adequate account of human action it is necessary to refer to the intentions with which some activity is done – without that we do not know *what* action has been done. Unless we know what story this action is a part of, we do not know what it is – it may of course be part of many stories. To have an intention is to be able to answer the question 'Why did you do that?' It is not necessary actually to ask and answer that question either with material words or by imagining the use of material words, but it is necessary to be prepared to answer it. To be prepared to tell the story of which your action was a part – this being so prepared is what having an intention *is*.

This means that questions about intentions only make sense in the case of animals *to whom* questions can be addressed. You can certainly speak of the reason why the dog chased a cat, but asking the dog about it does not enter into the matter. This is not because the dog happens to be dumb but because being non-linguistic it cannot have its *own* reasons; it cannot have intentions. This is why intentional action is the most thorough kind of self-moving, of auto-mobility, the highest kind of vitality or life. The highest kind of vitality belongs to the animal that has a life-story, not just a story that can be told about it, but a story it is capable of telling, a story that it actually enacts, a story it can tell itself.

The man who reviewed *Watership Down* in the *New York Review of Books* said that it was a pleasant story about some English children disguised as rabbits; and so it is. It has to be, because rabbits themselves cannot have stories. They have lifetimes but no life-stories. It is essential to a story that the course of events depends on the fulfilled or unfulfilled intentions of the protagonists. The protagonists have to be the kind of animals that are able to tell themselves the story in which they are engaged. Human living is enacted narrative – this is what differentiates the human animal from others.

The human animal is the one that in principle has an autobiography; to have an autobiography is the highest way of being an auto-mobile. I say 'in principle' because of course I can be a human being and happen to be incapable of providing my autobiography – I may be asleep, or too young to have acquired the language, or in some way handicapped; but that does not make a difference to the kind of animal to which I belong, the species I belong to. Other animals behave as they do because of the genetically determined structures that govern them; I can make choices because my actions are part of the story of which my life is the enactment, a story that I tell myself. Free choices and decisions are not random acts but carry on the story in one way or another. No animal makes a decision about how its lifetime is to be continued, in the sense that it might have been continued differently.

Human freedom, which is an aspect of human thinking, depends on, or rather consists in membership of the linguistic community, the world of symbols and linguistic, as distinct from sensual, meanings that are peculiar to the human animal. It consists in being a character in a story, your own story. But no stories, of course, are private. To be human and to have what we call a 'mind' is to belong in a particular way, a linguistic way, with other human animals. Every life-story has to be a shared life story and what characterizes the human way of living is that it is shared more than the living of other animals.

There could not be a clearer contrast between the Aristotelian kind of thinking and the Cartesian. For the Cartesian, consciousness is a way of being private; it belongs to an essentially hidden interior life; for the Aristotelian, thinking belongs to a world more social, in the sense of more *shared*, than any other. So long as, like other animals, I am restricted to sensual experience my life is private. No one can have *my* sensations; everyone can have my thoughts. If they could not they would not be thoughts. There is a special kind of conversation that we call discussion or argument which is a way of testing whether what I take to be my thoughts really are thoughts – they are not unless they can be shared by others. The use of language, then, is what frees us from imprisonment in the isolated itself; it is a way of transcending my individuality; to use the old jargon, it is a way of being 'immaterial'. The highest kind of auto-mobility of being spontaneous and self-originating is to transcend oneself, one's individuation, and this is what language consists in.

I want to conclude now with my third (most hurried and most enigmatic) section in which this self-transcendence is seen to be complete in grace, in sharing divine life. We have to begin with that primary usage of language, the life-story. No one, says St John, has ever seen God. Nearly all theological error comes from imagining that if we only knew the trick we could see God. Whatever could be seen in any sense of the word 'seen' could not be God. I do not just mean that God could not be a visible part of the material universe; I mean that God could not be conceptualized; there could not be any idea of God that we could contemplate. We know God as we know the author of an autobiography – and this I will suggest is a very odd business.

'No one has ever seen God,' says John, 'But the only son who is on the bosom of the Father he has' ... what? The Revised Standard Version (RSV) has 'he has made him known'. So does the English version of the Jerusalem Bible (JB). The original JB has 'l'a fait cognaitre'. I think these are all wrong. *Exegesato*, if Liddell and Scott are right, is best translated by the Latin Vulgate term *enarravit*. The old RC Douai/Rheims version gets it more or less right with 'declared', and the King James Authorized Version (as so often following Douai/Rheims) has 'declared', too. But *enarravit* is best. In the Prologue John first speaks of the Word, but then when the Word has been made flesh, he speaks only of the Son, and in this Son, God has become enacted narrative. *Exegeomai*, says Liddell and Scott, means to 'relate, to give a full account of'. That is, to tell the story – it is of course the word we get 'exegesis' from.

Anyway for John, what we have in the Word becoming flesh is a narrative and not a vision. Not a seeing but a listening to and sharing in a story. In becoming flesh the Word becomes a character in a story, a persona. In being made flesh the Word becomes a person, the 'Son' a distinct person from the 'Father' or 'he who sent'. The Word now has a distinct personality in the modern sense, with a different mind and will from the Father. 'Not my will but thine be done.'

The Word, so to say, in abstraction from the incarnation, the Word which is not historical narrative but simply the eternal divine Torah or Wisdom or God's concept of God is not another person than God, has no consciousness except the consciousness that is of the Godhead; just like the Spirit, God's delight in being God.

So the Word made flesh is Son, over against the Father. Over against because of the complex problems of authors and characters. Notice that as the Word becomes person over against the Father, the Father too enters the story but only, therefore, as a character, a persona, and so too does the Spirit.

For my immediate purpose it doesn't matter what you call an author; whether you think of an individual writer or of a culture or whatever. But let us for simplicity's sake be a little old-fashioned and speak of an individual author. The quest for the author looks simple at first sight: You just say 'Kenneth Grahame wrote *The Wind in the Willows*', but of course what you are doing then is simply telling another story in which one of the characters is called Kenneth Grahame. Kenneth Grahame has entered this story and become a *persona*, a character. Every accounting for a story, every exegesis, is telling another story. 'Every decoding is another encoding.' Very interesting problems arise if I say that I tell you the story that Kenneth Grahame told the story of *The Wind in the Willows*. These problems have to do with the fact that 'I' cannot function as a proper name. 'I tell you' is not part of a story in which 'I' is a character; it *is* the telling of a story. It is a sign of authority, of authorship as such (it is, as Aquinas would say, formal not material to the story). My life-story is not the story of 'I' but the story of Herbert McCabe, who has become a persona, a persona distinct from I, the author. As Herbert McCabe in the story I have been made flesh and dwell among the other characters. How do we get beyond any story to meet the ultimate author, the ultimate authority? May I draw your attention to the Irish or Anglo-Irish metaphysical narrative tradition – going from *Tristram Shandy*, through *At Swim Two Birds*, to Spike Milligan's *Puckoon*. In these the author seeks to enter the story he writes, partly in order that the reader may enter the story.

Laurence Sterne in *Tristram Shandy* is in ironic dialogue with his readers about how he is to write the novel which itself purports to be autobiography (the character is getting older, so is Sterne. The name was published in annual sections and is itself getting older; will the character ever catch up with himself as author?). But beyond that the reader knows there is a historical Laurence Sterne.

But how does he know this Laurence Sterne? Only by recognizing what you might call a Cloud of Unknowing.

Simply to know the author would be to put him in the novel and so it would not be to know him *as* author. Flann O'Brien carries the *TS* thing immensely further. In *At Swim*, besides being in dialogue with the reader about which of three possible openings we might have for the book, the novel itself is a purported autobiography of a man writing a novel about a novelist whose characters criticize him and persecute him and seek to kill him (to crucify him?). Then at a simpler level there is the character in *Puckoon* complaining, 'Did you write me these legs?'

And just to show that the thing isn't just Anglo-Irish, but Scottish-Jewish as well, in Muriel Spark's *The Comforters* the character Caroline Rose hears and resents the sound of Muriel Spark's typewriter making her life-story. More interestingly still, when Caroline comes to terms with being a character in a novel (the novel was written just after Spark's conversion to Catholicism) she begins to irritate the author who thus ceases to be Muriel Spark because she has entered the novel herself. Always beyond any such author-made character there is author-as-author, as Aquinas would say: the formal condition for there being a novel at all.

I am maintaining that autobiography does not take us to the author it is ostensibly about in the way that an ordinary story takes us to the character in the story. If the autobiographer tells us in his last chapter about beginning to write his autobiography this still does not do away with the unbridgeable gap between author-as-author and author-as-character. The difference, for example, between God as character in the Bible and God as author of the Bible, the difference, as Aquinas would say, between formal and material objects of faith. You only meet the author not in reading about him, but just in the story itself. This is of importance theologically because the Bible has to be seen as the autobiography of God, and the condition for reading the Bible as Bible is belonging to the people-of-God community in which alone the Bible exists as Bible. Then the Bible, the Word of God made history, the whole of it, is about Christ, the whole of it from Genesis to Apocalypse – it is, that is, if you regard it as Bible and not simply as Middle Eastern literature. To regard it as Bible is to read it in and with the community which sustains its existence. In David Lodge's *Small World*, you may remember, Persse McGarrigle on the spur of the moment switches the title of his Ph.D. thesis from 'The Influence of Shakespeare on T. S. Eliot' to 'The Influence of T. S. Eliot on Shakespeare'. For, of course, the Shakespeare we now have is ineluctably a Shakespeare existing in a sensibility moulded by, amongst others, Eliot. This doctrine of modern literary criticism ought to be very 'old hat' to Christian readers of the Bible: the Old Testament, for example, is heavily influenced by the New. The influence of T. S. Eliot on Shakespeare lies at the very root of at least Roman Catholic treatment of scripture. The scriptures exist in the contemporary historical community outside of which they may remain interesting but cease to be scripture.

I have argued elsewhere, and shall not here re-argue, that the historical life of Jesus is nothing but the Trinitarian life of God played out as history or projected onto our world.[1] There can be no life-story of the eternal God as such – to say 'eternal life' is to say non-narrative life, an incomprehensible concept – that is why no one has

1 See Herbert McCabe, *God, Christ and Us* (Continuum, London and New York, 2003), Chapter 20.

ever seen God, but the Son is his story. The point I leave you with now is that just as our human life consists in enacted narrative so our divine life is just our participation in the enacted narrative of God. The revelation of God to us is nothing except our being taken up into that narrative, the human story that is the sacrament or image of the unseen and unseeable, incomprehensible God.

Virtue and Truth

One of the difficulties we face in thinking about good and bad human behaviour in our culture is that we find it hard to grasp the notion of practical intelligence. We are so accustomed to the idea that intelligence is that by which we *discover* meaning in our world that we forget that it is also that by which we *impose* meaning on our world. This we do by intelligent, intentional action. A nineteenth-century admirer of Aristotle said 'Philosophers have sought to explain the world; the point is to change it'. That was, of course, Karl Marx. It was a point familiar to that earlier Aristotelian, Thomas Aquinas, who distinguishes theoretical and practical uses of reason. He does not suggest that the difference is a matter of what intelligence is concerned with – as though studying building techniques were somehow more practical than reading poetry. For him, both of these are exercises of the 'speculative' or theoretical intelligence. The distinction lies in what the intelligence is being used for: practical intelligence is exercised in actually making buildings, not in talking about them. For Aquinas, the study of human behaviour as human is, in itself, an exercise of the theoretical reason, but what it is about is people exercising practical reason: intelligence for getting something done.

For Aquinas, ethics is the analysis of human action in its full human reality. Happening to be a footballer or a dentist or a theologian is a kind of abstraction from the whole of you; you do not just *happen* to be human, being human is *what it takes for you to exist*. This analysis of human action *as* human is centrally about primarily intellectual disposition or skills, the virtue of right practical reason that Aquinas calls *prudentia*. It was later thinkers, many of them under the impression that they were followers of Thomas, who lost sight of practical intelligence and thought that we first exercised theoretical intelligence to deduce what is the right thing to do (the rules) and this was followed by a free and unpredictable *will* which decided whether to do it or not.

In this paper I would like first to give a brief account of how, as I understand the matter, we interpret our world, looking first at our *sensual* engagement with it and then that of our *understanding*. Here I do not think that we can avoid using *language* as a model for understanding. Human beings are linguistic animals, and to say this is to say that they have intelligence, a capacity for truth-grasping, even though intelligence is not identical with talking. Indeed, my central thesis is that we ought to pay much more attention than we commonly do to intelligence that is not displayed in speech. I would tentatively suggest that practical intelligence is the primary and even primitive form of intelligence and that we should think of the theoretical use of the intelligence by, as it were, a process of subtraction, rather than thinking of the practical use of intelligence by a process of addition to theoretical reason.

Aristotle thought that for a thing to be alive is for it to move itself. I shall now try to show how this proposition gives rise to the notion of meaning. Animals, including ourselves, are not social constructs like cars and conferences. They are *objectively*, in themselves, units – they need to be, so that they can be structured organisms. This

80

means that their parts are relevant to each other such that what goes on in one bit makes a difference to what goes on in the rest of the bits; what happens to or is done by one bit happens to or is done by the whole structure, the body. What happens in the dog's eye as the light reaches its retina happens to the whole dog and may cause it to move – its legs will move and this is for the whole dog to move. So in such a situation (which we call 'seeing') the whole dog (by its eyes) moves the whole dog (by its legs). The dog is moving itself; and this is for the dog to be living instead of inanimate. We do not say, literally, that the eye sees; we say that the dog sees with its eyes. We ought not to say that the eye sees and neither ought we to say that the brain sees, because seeing is not what happens in any special part of the dog but is the *relevance* of what happens in one part to what happens in other parts.

Relevance is not, of course, a material bit of an animal, though it only exists in material conditions. It is to do with the structure of an animal: what we call its 'nervous system'. What happens in the eye does not directly bring about a movement of the dog's feet; it brings about a *tendency* for the dog's feet to move, a tendency that exists among other tendencies. The complex sum of these tendencies, some cancelling others out, is the dog's behaviour. An animal can see if the light falling on its eye makes a difference to its behaviour. So we find out whether a particular kind of beetle has the sense of sight, not by trying to locate its eyes, but by finding out whether its behaviour in the dark is any different from its behaviour in the light.

An animal's behaviour, then, is dependent on its interpretation of the world, the meanings it finds in the world. For meaning is nothing but the place of a part in an organized structure. When an animal finds a meaning it makes an evaluation of its world; one that is necessary for its survival and the survival of its species. It needs to see some parts of its world as edible, some as dangerous, some as sexually attractive, and to take appropriate action. Without such genetically built-in evaluations and tendencies it would speedily be destroyed and have few if any progeny. This is what natural selection is about.

So to engage sensually with the world is to find meaning or value in it. This meaning is located in the material nervous system of this particular individual beast. It is the meaning of its world for, let us say, this particular sheep, a meaning which is individual and incommunicable. No other sheep can have exactly the same sensual meaning to its world, though animals of the species or gene pool may be expected to have very similar sensual interpretations of the world. No other animal of my species could have my identical sensual experiences any more than it could kick with my foot. Sensations are private, individual and located in my body. I stress this to contrast such experience of sensual meaning with the organization of sensual meanings as linguistic meanings, by which we make concepts which are the meaning of symbols and especially words. How an animal evaluates and interprets its world sensually is determined genetically by the structure of its nervous system with which it was born. The *potential* sense-meaning which lies dormant in the chemical and biological structure of material things around the animal is so to say woken and actualized by these structures being taken up into the structure of the animal's inherited nervous system. Animals raise the structures or forms of material things to the dignity of sensual meanings. Human animals (uniquely) go on to raise such sensual meanings to the dignity of concepts – linguistic meanings.

I want to suggest that we look on our capacity for understanding as a capacity, shared by the whole species, for creating a structure analogous to the nervous system, but shared by a group and in principle shareable by the whole species: this is language. Then, just as the structure of the nervous system is the location of sensual interpretations, so language is the 'location', so to say, of intelligible interpretations. The vital difference, however, is that even if our *capacity* for language is genetically provided (and there are serious difficulties about explaining how this could have developed by ordinary natural selection) and even though, like very many of our fellow-animals, we are born with an instinctive set of signals that we call 'body-language', we are not born with English or even Irish or any language in the strict sense, any particular structure of conventional signs. And all languages are particular structures of signs. Such structures are not evolved but developed by tradition in the history of particular groups of linguistic animals.

This is not a modern concern: it puzzled the people who write in *Genesis* about the tower of Babel (and compare the account of Pentecost in the New Testament). We are born with a capacity to *create* and *learn* language; we are not born with a language. There is, however, a sense in which all human languages, although produced separately, are potentially one – in that all are, in principle, intertranslatable. Moreover, as I have said, just as our non-linguistic fellow-animals are genetically provided with a repertoire of signals which form a basis of social life (and which some people mistake for linguistic communication) so we too inherit certain spontaneous gestures common to our whole species, though in our case they are modified and merge into our linguistic behaviour in the form of 'body language'. I shall not rehearse here Wittgenstein's (I think) wholly convincing demolition of the idea of a 'private language', the notion that the meanings of my words are located inside my head and may not be available for inspection by others, rather as my sensations *are* a function of my individual nervous system. Wittgenstein does not deny that I *have* concepts in my own mind, a capacity which is part of the life of this individual human body. He simply denies that such concepts could be, for me, the *meaning* of my words. Rather, a concept is a skill in using a word which has its meaning from its part in the structure of the language. If words have their meaning 'in the language' which does not belong to any material individual, any body, but to everybody, then linguistic meanings are not individual material things or functions of individual material brains, and the capacity to deploy meanings is not a capacity for any individual bodily process as sensation is.

The fact that meanings, unlike sensations, are nobody's private property means that when we share the same language, you do not have a *similar* meaning for a word to the one that I have (as your *sensations* might be similar to mine). You have the *identical* idea that I have. If we have different ideas and are at cross-purposes this will soon become evident and can easily be corrected.

Now a word about appetites. We have a capacity to be attracted by the world as we interpret it. The interpretation in question may be *sensual* (and this we share with our non-linguistic fellow-animals) or it may be *intellectual* or

84

linguistic. In either case the proximate cause of the attraction is not precisely in what we *are* but in what we *know*. If I lift up a smallish dog and then let go, it will fall to the ground, be attracted to the ground, because of what it *is* (heavier than air). But if the dog sees a rabbit the chances are it will set off in pursuit, and this attraction will be because of what it knows (sensually, of course). It is running *because* it has *seen* the rabbit.

Unlike our fellow animals, we are *also* attracted to a bit of the world because of the intellectual interpretation that we give to it – which is to say, it is as though we were talking about it to ourselves. We are attracted because of something we can 'say' about it. A healthy, hungry dog confronted by a juicy steak is attracted, and cannot be other than attracted, and will act on the attraction and go for the steak, unless it has been specially trained not to – and then it cannot do other than (however reluctantly) *not* act on the attraction. Whatever the dog does is what it cannot do other than, in the circumstances; there are no other possibilities. However, when I am healthy and hungry and confronted by a juicy steak, I may be attracted to it in much the same way as the dog; but I may also be attracted or otherwise because I tell myself about the steak. I can be attracted (or not) by the steak under some *description*: 'It belongs to someone else'; 'It is full of cholesterol'; 'It was made by slaughtering harmless beasts'; 'It is expensive' ... This list could go on indefinitely, and that is the root of my freedom. When I act because of such a linguistic interpretation of the world it was always possible for me to have acted differently. It is a fundamental characteristic of language that it can express what is-but-might-not-have-been. It is because, unlike our non-linguistic fellow-animals, we can be attracted or repelled by something not only under some aspect (like its taste or smell or sexual allure) but also under a *description*, that what we decide to do is a matter of free choice.

Like St Augustine, St Thomas speaks of free choice or decision (*liberum arbitrium*) and not, as later writers did, of free will. For the later writers, freedom was a mysterious property of the will. For Aquinas, the will is, of course, operative in choice, but the choice is free because the will is our capacity to be attracted by what is *understood* to be in some way good. So, unless confronted by sheer goodness itself, which is God (whom, in any case, we cannot understand in this life), the will may have a rich variety of possible reasons for being attracted; and there is no such thing as the only one; and so our choice or decision (*electio*) is free. For Aquinas we are free, not because we act at random or unpredictably, but because we act for reasons and there are many possible available reasons. Which reasons we are likely to plump for to motivate our action has to do, I shall suggest, with what we have made of ourselves – our virtues and vices.

When Aristotle talks of choice, *prohairesis*, he speaks of exercising an 'appetitive intelligence' or an 'intelligent appetite'. For Aquinas, this applies to every phase in human action. In the exercise of practical reason at no point are intellect and will separated. There is no act of practical intelligence which is not also one of will, and vice versa. Aquinas likes to say that the two are not like two powers side by side, but are united as are form and matter, though frequently interchanging these roles.

In order to understand the context for Aquinas's account of human action it is necessary to say something about dispositions (what he calls *habitus*). I shall try to be brief here because the topic has been well-aired at least since Gilbert Ryle published *The Concept of Mind* in 1949 and restored it to its proper prominence in the philosophy of psychology, and especially since Alasdair MacIntyre in *After Virtue* in 1981 showed the disastrous effects of neglecting it in moral philosophy.

A game such as football imposes two different kinds of limitation on its players: they should play the game well and they should not cheat. The first is concerned with dispositions (skills), the second with particular acts and rules. Learning how to play well is analogous to acquiring a virtue; cheating is not playing the game badly: it is not playing it at all, it is attempting to be adjudged a winner by an action which is not part of the game at all but pretends to be, and is analogous to sin.

A certain kind of law which absolutely prohibits certain acts has the function of listing various common ways of cheating. Such laws define the boundaries of the game. From the point of view of moral *philosophy*, the game is human friendship in the sense in which Aristotle (*Politics* III, 9) described it as the fundamental relationship by which people are fellow-citizens, which is greater than the justice one must extend even to non-citizens.

This friendship (*philia*) involves participation in a common task: a concern for each other's flourishing, which implies a concern for their growth in the virtues needed for human happiness. (There is a fashion at the moment, amongst those who believe in what they call the 'market economy', for what Aristotle would regard as treating fellow-citizens as though they were all foreigners.) From the point of view of moral *theology*, the *philia* in question which defines the human game is *agape* or *caritas*, the friendship that God shares with us and enables us to share with each other.

A table of prohibitions, such as the Decalogue, defines the boundaries of *caritas*. To break them is not a matter of playing the game poorly but of stepping outside the field of play. To remedy this situation you do not need to learn to play better, to acquire further skill; you need to hope for forgiveness and a gratuitous invitation to return. Of course, whether in the game of football or of life, being thoroughly familiar with such laws does not help you to play well – indeed, it is quite compatible with not playing the game at all. It is an exercise not of practical but of theoretical intelligence.

To play the game well we need not rule books but training. We may at first make use of training manuals or teachers, but we do not acquire the skill we need by reading the books or listening to the teachers. We do so by practising in accordance with their teaching. Practising has a twofold effect: you acquire an insight into the demands of the situation you are in and, simultaneously, become more attracted to dealing with it in the best way. As you get better at playing you become more enthusiastic about the game. This is the combined operation of practical intelligence and will.

Of course, acquiring a skill is not the same as acquiring a virtue for two reasons: in the first place, skill is concerned with the good of what is *produced* (a good move in football or an excellent painting or whatever) whereas a virtue is concerned with the excellence of the *producer*. The second difference is that skills are acquired *only* by practice (although some people may be genetically provided with certain natural gifts which make it easier for them to acquire a particular skill – think of Mozart or Pascal). Virtues, however, which enable us to live the life of *caritas*, which is the life of God, life in the Spirit, although they encourage us to more intensive practice, are not rooted in *our* efforts but in the initiative of God. This is implied in God sharing his life with us. The result is what is traditionally called 'infused' as distinct from 'acquired' virtue. The divine, or so-called 'theological' virtues of faith, hope and charity can only be infused through the gift of the Spirit, but this grace also gives a new dimension, and indeed transformation, to our *acquired* virtues. As Aquinas puts it, the charity we have been given becomes the form of all our virtues and our whole life becomes a sharing in divinity.

Of course we can acquire vices as well as virtues and with these, in a parallel way, practice makes imperfect. However, in so far as I know, nobody has spoken of 'infused vices'. Either way, our acquisition of such dispositions forms for us our character or personality, the kind of person we are. This is extremely important for Aquinas's account of decisive human action, and Aristotle says that without a formed character (whether good or bad) *prohairesis*, free choice, is not possible. Children can have whims and stick to them stubbornly. But this is not the same as decisive action. We can, of course, do good or bad acts without having yet acquired the virtues or vices which would make such conduct 'second nature' to us (how else could we acquire these dispositions?) just as we can play chess or football before we become expert at it. Nevertheless, until we have acquired the dispositions that form our personality as part of that personality, our action does not spring from the depth of us.

It is not done for the love of a certain way of being alive, of delight in being ourselves. And to this extent it is less our own – to this extent less free.

This means that if we act because we happen to know that we have a duty to do so and not out of an inclination to do so (because of the sort of person we have become) then we are *not* living well. It would be hard (short of hedonism) to get further away from Kant's position; for (arguably) he would regard acting out of inclination as diminishing the value of an act which ought to be done from an uncontaminated sense of duty. We ought, of course, to be clear that acting from the inclination arising from virtue does not mean taking the easiest or least painful path. It means taking the one that conforms to and springs from who you are and what you treat as ultimately satisfactory.

Only people whose ultimate end was set in pleasure and comfort (infantile, intemperate people) would mean by their deepest personal inclination always the easiest path. Although (as is not the case with the modern word 'habit' – as in 'a habit of smoking', 'a drinking habit'), a *habitus* (as Aquinas, for example, understands it) makes it easier to do what you want to do, not harder not to do what you don't want to do. Nevertheless, you do not do something out of a *habitus* like, say, justice, *because* it is *easier* but because it is what you really want to do. Those with the virtue of justice act not because they find it easier to be just, but because their will, their love, is set on justice. Those who lack the virtue of justice may, indeed, do what is just, but they will do so, not from the love of justice, but from, for example, fear of retribution, human or divine. They are, to this extent, less free. Freedom, as I understand it, has two conditions: first a free act is one which in the same circumstances might have been different, and second that it has its origin in the agent and not in some coercive power. To act from the personality you have built for yourself or which has been given to you by God's grace, or both, is to act in total freedom, to act from yourself.

A free human action begins with intending to achieve some desired end – drinking a pint of Guinness, let us say. Intending to do this is not simply recognizing that you like Guinness or that Guinness is good for you; it is being attracted by Guinness presented to your mind as an immediate possibility: there are ways of getting some here and now.

Intending, in this sense, is not an act in the modern sense of a deed but rather an *actus* in the medieval sense of the actualization of some potentiality. What is made actual in this case is a state or condition of intending; it is setting the stage for deliberation and decision. It is more like being awake than like the act of waking up. Once the stage is set I may start to consider how I shall set about achieving my purpose. There may be no problem about this – if, for example, someone sets a bottle and a glass before me. But quite often there seem to be many different routes to my objective. The intellectual virtue of practical wisdom, prudence (*prudentia*), is concerned with judging well among these means not only as effective for the end but also as appropriate to me. The scope of *prudentia* is the exercise of practical reason as shaped by the attractiveness of the end I have in view.

Anthony Kenny has pointed out that the logic of practical reasoning differs from that of theoretical reasoning.[1]

1 See Anthony Kenny, *Will, Freedom, and Power* (Oxford, 1975), Chapter 5.

In valid theoretical reasoning the truth of the conclusion follows *necessarily* from the truth of the premises, and if this is established the truth of the conclusion will then be quite unaffected by *further true premises* that might be added. Practical reasoning about the means by which I might achieve the end I have in view differs from theoretical reasoning in both these respects. Typically such reasoning goes: I want to go to London; this train is going there; so I'll take it. In the first place, the conclusion is not necessary; I could go by car or plane or walk. It would be *sufficient* to take the train since it is going to London, but other means would also be sufficient. I decide between these various sufficient means by taking into account other factors. In other words (and this is the second difference) the addition of *further true premises* in practical reasoning does make a difference to the conclusion I come to. So I have to consider whether the train might not be delayed by leaves or snow, that it will take me to Paddington, which would not be convenient ... etc.

Spotting and judging the importance of such extra factors is more than can be done by the intellect alone. It involves a sensual involvement with the world and is the fruit of considerable sense-experience. It follows that practical reason is not a *scientia* (science) in the sense of conclusions arrived at and seen to be necessary because they can be traced back to first principles. Because, as Aquinas repeatedly insists, human actions are particular and concrete they are not susceptible to a deductive analysis. In the end the guarantee of the trustworthiness of practical judgements and the validity of moral judgements lies not in any code but in the verdict of good, experienced, wise people.

This is not to say that there is no certainty at all in moral generalizations. If I may go back for a moment to the distinction between playing football badly and committing a foul: just how well someone has played may be a matter for debate, but if the relevant facts are clear then it is equally clear whether a move was or was not within the *boundaries* of football. One overriding extra factor in judging whether a course of action is suitable as a means to my end is whether it amounts to a foul, whether it would be incompatible with the *caritas* that defines the playing field. In other words there is a place within an ethics of virtue for absolute prohibitions as there is a place in football for the referee's whistle.

I hope it will be evident how very different this account of human action (which I believe to be faithful to St Thomas) is from the scholastic development of the 'Manuals of Moral Theology'. For that line of thinking, intellect or reason and will are quite separate and even opposed faculties. The right reason of which they sometimes speak is a theoretical use of reason which gives an account of what is implied by basic laws. It is an often fascinating study in the refinement of the rules, but it ends up with *propositions* stating the rules that ought to be followed. When the manuals are printed and distributed it is then a matter for the reader to use his will-power to obey these rules – often with the ingenious guidance of casuists who, full of human compassion, refine the rules still more, but they are still general rules. The manuals show no serious interest in the development of Christian life, the growth in grace by which people are educated in the moral dispositions, virtues, so that they mature into being their true selves. In place of the truth involved in Aquinas's account of action (recognition of relevant factors in the judgement of means and the discovery of the self in decision) there is an appeal simply to obedience – thought to be the work of a quite unpredictable and almost random free will. For Aquinas, by contrast, the basis of the moral life is *prudentia*, right practical reason in the development of *caritas*; an intellectual virtue which cannot be *exercised* without the moral virtues, and which cannot be exercised *effectively* without the infused divine virtues.

Prudentia is concerned not just with deliberation but with the 'operative syllogism' in which one premise derives from an insight into a single concrete material individual ('I am this character in this life-story under these circumstances'), something which cannot (for any Aristotelian) be grasped by intellect alone; for intellect deals through meaningful signs such as words, and an individual thing can never be the meaning of a word. The mind, for Aquinas, can only cope with the material individual by reflection on, and insight into, the way in which this human animal acquired its repertoire of meanings through its sensual experience (as organized by the 'interior senses': the *sensus communis*, the *imaginatio*, the sense *memoria* and the *vis cogitativa*), all of which are a bodily affair. So the virtue that is developed in the practical reason demands more than abstract understanding; practical wisdom is developed not just by reading, talking or arguing but by imagination, imagery and stories, by experience; it demands bodily sensitivity to the world around us. It may be worth repeating the familiar reminder that Thomas Aquinas does not know of 'moral theology'. He has simply an account of the stumbling journey of the return of human animals to God, as creatures to their creator, and as sinners to their forgiving healer.

Animals and Us

One of our great recent cultural achievements has been the rapid development of ethology, the study of the behaviour of non-human animals. I remember coming across the memoirs of a Victorian clergyman in which he tells us that looking out of the window one morning he saw a, to him, totally strange and wonderful bird. He describes its brilliant plumage, and its grace and beauty, as being like nothing he had ever seen before. But then he says: 'However, while I went to get my gun it flew away.' I think we could say that that sentence could not be seriously written by anyone today – not even a clergyman. And this is almost entirely due to the growth in our understanding. We know so much more now about the sheer intricacy of animal behaviour that we look on it, if not with awe, at least with proper respect. The notion that, unless domesticated, animals are 'wild' and can be expected to be savage and dangerous has slipped quietly away. In proper and predictable circumstances animals will attack us either in hunting or in defence but, by a very large margin we are more likely to be attacked by members of our own species. (We should frequently call to mind that in English law an oyster is a wild animal whereas a human being is not.)

One of the things we have found out is that many non-human animals live in societies, and we know quite a lot about how these societies are structured. We also understand more clearly than our ancestors did that animals can fall in love, rejoice and grieve, and have real devotion to each other, and so on. Of course people have told stories about animals for centuries, usually, but not always, moral allegories. But in our generation when it has (I shall argue) become clear that one thing an animal cannot be is a character in a story, we know with some precision how their emotional lives develop. And, of course, it seems likely that we shall know a great deal more as time goes on.

I shall also try to argue that one development that has not been so happy is the growth of talk about 'animal rights'. I regard this as a muddle, and a counter-productive one. If you base your case for treating animals kindly (and trying to avoid causing them unnecessary pain) on the notion of animal rights, then if people come to recognize that this is a non-concept there will be nothing left to base your case on. I shall try to convince you that cruelty to animals, which plays such a large part in the economy of modern human society, is not contrary to the virtue of justice but of temperance. As I see it, the reduction of temperance to justice is as mistaken as its twentieth-century shadow or mirror image: 'emotivism', which seeks to reduce justice to temperance.

There is undoubtedly in our time a much greater awareness of the evil of cruelty to animals than was shown in earlier times. There is, so far as I know only one reference in the whole of the *Summa Theologiae* to cruelty to animals, and this comes not in a discussion of the virtue of temperance but in the treatment of the ceremonial precepts of the Old Law concerning eating and drinking and sacrifice. Here St Thomas hazards a guess that the kosher rule against butchering animals by strangulation may have arisen because the practice would be too cruel to the beast. But he is careful to add that it was forbidden because the cruelty to other animals might overflow into cruelty to people. Elsewhere in Aquinas, *crudelitas* (cruelty,

96

a vice opposed to *temperantia*, temperance) is invariably cruelty to people, and usually in the context of punishment. Like the US Constitution, Aquinas disapproved of 'cruel and unusual punishments' (though to his mind that might easily include the electric chair).

Our concern with cruelty to animals arises from an increased awareness of our solidarity with fellow sensitive beings. We feel that foxhunting and cockfighting are obscene and degrading, and if we legislate against them it is not because we are concerned with the alleged rights of foxes or hens, but because despite our liberalism we still retain some sense that the state has a responsibility for the virtue and maturity and happiness of its citizens. So far as I know we are the only animal species that keeps pets. This is not the same as making *use* of other species (which is to be found, for example, in all parasites). The difference lies in the emotional bond that arises with pets.

I need now to look at the parallels and differences between the social and emotional life of non-human animals and human ones, which I am going to treat as the parallels and differences between a life which is purely sensitive and one in which sensitivity is intensified and transcended in language.

For these purposes I shall first of all have to argue against a mechanical model of sensitive life such as became dominant in Europe during the seventeenth century and which still has a certain lingering respectability. So the first thing I have to argue is that animals are not machines. The second thing I shall have to argue is that animals do not have understanding. I am going to treat understanding as a capacity for using language – though 'language' here has a rather broad sense.

Looming over and dominating what I have to say will be a certain imaginative model: the model of a network – in fact, two networks. The first network or structure I shall label the nervous system: without some notion of this the sensitive life is, I think, unintelligible. The second network is that of language: without some notion of this the intellectual life is unintelligible. The human, linguistic animal operates and lives in terms of both interacting networks; our non-linguistic fellow-animals live in terms only of the first. For many species of non-linguistic animals, their nervous system, though not identical, is strikingly similar to ours – so much so that ethology, the study of their behaviour, throws valuable light on our own.

What I mean by a network is a complex unified system in which what happens in one part is relevant to what happens in other parts. The parts of a network are, as it were, instruments operating on other parts. So we can speak of a network as 'organic' (from the Greek word for an instrument, *organon*).

Of course we can *construct* such a network: this is what we do when we institute an organization – the United Nations, for example. But there are special organic networks which only *exist* in virtue of being networks. These are alive. This is not true of the United Nations, which consists of parts (people, for example) which already existed before being organized into this network. If and when the organization is disbanded, we *may* speak of it having 'died' or 'gone out of existence'. But, in fact, nothing will literally have gone out of existence. The people in it, together with their various equipments, will carry on as before – only no longer accidentally arranged in relation to each other in the way they were previously. We therefore speak only metaphorically when we say that the organization has died. And the metaphor is taken from plants and animals whose *existence* does consist in the organic network structure of their parts.

Aquinas speaks of an organization such as this one as an '*ens per accidens*' (which does not, by the way, mean the same thing as an 'accident'). That is to say it is an '*ens*', an existing being, only by courtesy of our convenience and our language. We happen to have a single name for the United Nations, so for convenience we treat it as one existent thing when really it is the incidental coming together of many existent things which it is convenient to *treat* as a unity but which does not have the real unity of, say, a cow or a tree. When a cow is conceived something very drastic happens. A new thing comes into existence. Similarly, something very drastic happens when an old cow dies and goes out of existence. If, however, you make a model cow out of, say, matchsticks, nothing so drastic happens. In the same way, it is convenient for our purposes to group the stars of the heavens in constellations (with fancied resemblances to characters in Greek mythology); but these constellations do not exist as units *of themselves*. They are beings only '*per accidens*'. As a matter of fact, nearly all the nouns and noun-phrases in our language signify *entia per accidens*, like the United Nations, and not *entia per se*, like the cow which exists precisely in virtue of being a cow.

There is, in other words, a correlation, but not a direct correlation, between the structure of reality, the actual things that there are, and the structure of our language. That is why chemists and physicists and other scientists have to construct special technical language to supplement ordinary language. Philosophers called 'nominalists' hold that there is no structure in reality itself, that all structure is imposed by the shape of our language: the nouns we happen to have determine the boundaries of the things we think there are. I think the whole progress of Western science is itself a refutation of this view: scientists, for the most part, believe they are getting at some truth about the way things actually are. Nevertheless this is a laborious task because, as I have said, there is no direct correlation between the structure of reality and the structure of the language we have devised, not for expressing the true structure of the world, but for the practical purpose of coping with it.

A machine is an imitation animal and, especially since the developments in computer technology, we can make this imitation as close as we like; and one use for such a machine is to throw light on the structure and function of real animals. Nevertheless an animal itself is not a machine. And the fundamental reason for this is that an animal belongs to a *species*. Belonging to a species is not simply belonging to a logical class. You can make up a logical class, if you like, of all those pieces of aluminium that are less than four metres high and moving at more than two kilometres to the hour. But an animal species (e.g. all the tigers there ever were) is not such an arbitrary grouping. It is a material thing – an unusual material thing, in that it does not all exist at one time, but nonetheless a material thing that comes into existence by natural selection at a certain time and (with the possible exception of cockroaches) will go out of existence again by natural selection at a later time. In order to be a real sheep it is not enough to resemble other sheep, however closely: you have to be born of other sheep. A species is in one sense made up of individuals, but in a more important sense the individual is made by the species. Most of what we understand about a sheep is understood because we see it in its species, in its genetic context. In order to be a real human being the Son of God had to be born of Mary.

Now we can put a machine resembling a sheep in a science museum to illustrate the functioning of a real sheep. But this is just one individual machine constructed by us, and constructed by *us* because *we* and we alone live not only in virtue of the kind of network which defines the life of, say, a sheep, but also in a second network of language. When a sheep is brought into existence by other sheep it is not *constructed*. The pattern according to which it comes into existence is, as they say (metaphorically) 'inscribed' in its genes, not, as with the construction of a machine, inscribed within the language of the maker.

But, of course, at enormous expense we could, it seems, make a machine which not only resembled a real sheep so closely as to deceive even the elect, but also imitated all those processes by which the sheep (together with another sheep) reproduces and produces progeny. I see no reason, offhand, why we should not be able to waste money in this way. But if we do, we shall not have made an imitation animal but an actual animal species. The thing we shall have made will no longer need to be constructed by what I shall shortly be calling 'rational creatures' (who live in and by the second network). It will be an ordinary dumb beast coming into existence because of the species. (The museum would find it a lot cheaper to buy an ordinary sheep.)

One of the reasons, quite apart from the expense, why it might be inadvisable to make an animal species in this way is that we don't know enough about animals to be sure that it would be safe. We are already beginning to have worries about life that is merely *modified* by genetic engineering; it would clearly be a good deal more dicey to make a totally new species out of whole cloth. Once we have constructed it it ceases to be under our control. Nevertheless, the philosophical interest is in the possibility of so doing. I can see no logical difficulty about human animals constructing artificial animals except the logical difficulty that from the second generation onwards they would no longer be artificial animals but ordinary real ones – not the product of our skill but of their parents' genes. How they would get on ecologically, that is to say as a functioning part of what I'm afraid I would call the 'meta-network', in which different species relate to each other, is something we know almost nothing about, and which may even be in principle unpredictable.

From Plato through Augustine to Descartes, people have had a nearly irresistible desire to claim that human beings are not one being but two. This claim is commonly referred to as *dualism*. According to this, there is, on the one hand, the body, which seems obvious enough; and there is also the soul, which is invisible and presents greater problems. In this view corruption, perishability and death belong to the body, but it is inhabited by a spiritual soul which is invisible because it is non-material; and some dualists (in fact all three I just mentioned) say that this soul, being non-material and not subject to decay and decomposing as the body is, is immortal and survives the death of the body. For these people the soul is the *real* me, so I can be immortal even after the body dies. Other people, like Aristotle and Thomas Aquinas, said that this is not so. Aquinas says that after death my soul may be in heaven 'but my soul is not me' (*anima mea non est ego*). They said that I am one thing. I am this living material body, just as any other animal is a living material body. They were happy to speak of the soul (for Aristotle, the *psyche* and for Aquinas, the *anima*) but this for them does not *inhabit* the body. It is first of all the actual life of the body. For them the body *is* a body, a living body as distinct from a corpse (which is a collection of other bodies) because it is alive, and being alive just is having a soul. For other animals to be alive is to have in varying degrees a functioning nervous system (network 1). And this is to have such vital activities as sensation, emotions, desires, pain, grief, cheerfulness, loneliness and affection. By vital activities I mean *behaviour* as distinct from simply what happens to an animal, like slipping on a banana skin or getting wet in the rain. Now human animals are in the same position but more so.

I shall be suggesting in a moment that what I have been speaking of, which is the sensitive life, is fundamentally a matter of finding *meaning* in the world surrounding the animal. So a word now about meaning. Once we have the notion of the organic network in which each part is relevant to other parts we can make use of the notion of meaning; the meaning of a bit of a network is the part it plays in the whole unified network. If you want to explain what a Member of Parliament is you have to explain the part he or she plays in the parliamentary system. If you want to explain what the meaning of the word 'perhaps' or 'troglodyte' or 'facilitate' is, you have to explain what part these words play in the system of the English language. That is what dictionaries tell you. Now to live in virtue of having a functioning nervous system is to interpret the world around you by, so to say, taking it up into the meaning-pattern of this network such that what goes on in your various sensors (your skin, your eyes, your nose) is relevant or meaningful for the operation of your hands and feet and jaws, and vice versa. By the sensitive life you interpret your environment as significant for you. This bit is edible, this is sexually attractive, this is dangerous, and so on. And your behaviour with respect to your surroundings is mediated by this interpretation. Animals behave because of how they sensually interpret their world.

To be alive, for Aristotle and Aquinas, is first of all to be self-moving. But self-movement is not possible for a machine, though we may make a machine to simulate it. A machine cannot move itself because it is not a single self but a collection of things each of which may exist of itself but is only accidentally associated with the other bits. Whereas an eye detached from the body does not exist as an eye. An eye is said to see (which is a vital activity) because what goes on in the eye, which is essentially part of the animal (exists as an *eye* by being part of the animal) affects what goes on in the legs, which are also essentially part of the same animal. And the animal exists by having, as essential organic parts, eyes and legs and so on. So what goes on in the eye goes on in the animal and what goes on in the legs goes on in the same animal, so that the animal moves the animal. It is self-moving.

The possibility of sensitive life depends on the natural (non-simulated) unity of the organic structure of the living organic body. A machine which is, you might say, a group of instruments for *us*, pretending to be a unity (made of instruments for *itself*), *simulating* an animal, does not interpret the world and thus does not act purposefully as real animals do. The dog runs because it sees the rabbit.

For the dualist the body is a machine and what goes on in the eye is seeing because there is some kind of connection between the body and what dualists call a consciousness or mind or (in extreme cases) a 'self'. It is hard for the dualist to give an account of this connection between the two things that make me up.

Consistently and rigorously maintained, such a dualism also has to deny that an animal can see, just as most of us would deny that one of those devices that opens the door for you as you leave a supermarket can actually see you approaching. For a dualist, seeing as we do and feeling as we do would have to belong exclusively to beings like us who have a subjective consciousness as well as an objective body. A logically very similar version of dualism, which is much more popular these days, is the idea that what sees is the brain. The eye, ears and nose send what are obscurely called 'messages' to the brain, which acts like a vast and immensely complex computer. I would argue that this model, useful though it often is, collapses because computers don't sort anything out. They are used by *people* to sort things out.

I want to maintain that what makes the impact of light on, say, the cow's retina count as *seeing* is the organic coordination of the bits of the cow's body. So the cow's eye does not see. Nor does its brain see. The cow sees. And the cow is not something standing over against and separate from the cow's body. It just is this naturally organized unitary body. We do not need, to use Gilbert Ryle's language, to postulate a 'ghost in the machine'. We need to observe that an animal is not a machine at all. (Actually, the French Thomist, Jacques Maritain, got in some decades earlier than Gilbert Ryle's *Concept of Mind*, though his phrase for Descartes's notion of the human animal was 'the angel in the machine'.)

So the network of sensitivity which I have called network 1 provides animals, including ourselves, with a pattern of meaning in our world, which I shall call *sensual* meaning. For medieval thinkers like Albert the Great and Thomas Aquinas, this sensual life was enormously richer than anything conceived of by the empiricists of the seventeenth and later centuries, with their talk of 'sense data', in which a kind of picture in the head reproduces the appearance of the world before you. The organization of the world in terms of meaning, the first animal interpretation of the world, belongs for these *pre*-Cartesian thinkers to the organized body, to the sphere of the senses. For Aquinas there are nine senses: besides the five exterior ones, there is the *sensus communis* which coordinates the deliveries of these senses to form a gestalt, a meaningful pattern; there is the *imaginatio* which enables us to recall what it was like to sense; the *sensus aestimativus* or evaluative sense which estimates what's in it for the animal's life; and the *sense memory* of particular events. All this is before any understanding takes place.

When the human animal appears on the scene the extraordinary (and so far inexplicable) thing that happens is the emergence of language. Language is a network of symbols that makes us able to interpret objectively the subjective sensual interpretation of the world. Language is a network in which the world has meaning not simply by being taken up into the complex pattern of the bodily nervous system but into a new pattern of symbols which is constructed by the linguistic animal itself. The nervous system (network 1) is genetically provided: the DNA which initiates and partially determines the structure of the body is supplied by parents. The structure of the brain and the rest of the system is biologically inherited. But language is not. Language is a product, a set of conventional signs, an *artefact*. And it is what makes *all* artefacts possible. The precondition for language, the enormous degree of complexity in the human nervous system is, of course, biologically provided, though it is not at all clear how this could have happened by the familiar evolutionary process of natural selection. (Just as, at the other end, it is plainly incoherent to speak of the first life as having evolved. Natural selection is a process within plant or animal life in reproducing itself. You can't have evolution in any Darwinian sense until you already have reproductive organic life.)

Aquinas thought that one of Aristotle's greatest contributions, among very many, to human thought was to clearly distinguish sensation (the sensual interpretation of the world) from understanding (the intellectual linguistic interpretation of the world). I would say that the greatest sin of the empiricists against human thought was to go back to the old pre-Aristotle muddle – mainly through not understanding what language is. But I'd better not go into that now.

The capacity to use an agreed system of symbols to express what our world is, is *our* kind of understanding. This capacity makes the human animal not simply a different species of animal but an animal in a new sense, having life in a new sense. It is because language is created by the human animal, and not biologically inherited, that he or she has life, has self-movement, in a new sense, has freedom. With the appearance of the linguistic animal evolution becomes largely irrelevant. Natural selection is, after all, an astonishingly cumbersome mode of change: since the life of the parent cannot have any effect on the genes that it passes on to its progeny. Alteration in the genes is not due to the kind of life the parent lives or anything it learns, but simply to chance mutations, most of which are bad for its offspring, although a tiny minority may by good luck turn out to be useful or, as they say, *adaptive* to new conditions.

With the coming of the linguistic animal, however, evolution is replaced by history and *tradition* which is just the inheritance (not biological but social) of acquired characteristics. The linguistic animal can adapt itself within its own lifetime and by language transmit the new art or technology or wisdom to the next generation. This is very much quicker and more efficient than natural selection.

There is, of course, an unfortunate corruption of the English language by which people speak of almost any change over time, any development, as an 'evolution'. People speak of the evolution of atomic theory or of Christian doctrine or even of the universe itself. But this can only lead to confusion and muddle. Evolution means Darwin or it means nothing.

Animal behaviour of any kind is a matter of being attracted or repelled by what it interprets of its world. This is *orexis* or appetite. If the animal interprets the world *sensually* it is moved by sensual appetites like hunger and fear and sexual stimulation and, especially with the young of sophisticated animals, the desire for fun. The linguistic animal is, in a parallel way, moved by its linguistic or rational interpretation of its world.

An absolutely fundamental feature of the language network is its capacity to express what is-but-might-not-be and thus also what is-not-but-might-be. Non-linguistic animals can be puzzled, bewildered and surprised, but the nervous system (network 1) provides no way of expressing this except by symptoms, e.g. trembling, or whining, or whatever. (In a similar way, as Aquinas puts it, a dumb animal acts for a reason and acts *voluntarie* or *involuntarie* (willingly or unwillingly) but it does not *have* the reason as its *own* nor the willing as its own.) But the linguistic animal has the capacity to ask questions and answer them, to envisage the possibility of what is not. The negation sign is the heart of language. The answering of asked questions is the basis of *truth and falsity* and is the reason why language is objective and not merely subjective and individual as sensations are. Your sensations belong to *your* individual body and mine to *my* body. They may be similar because we are both the same kind of animal, but they are individaul and private property. The meaning of a piece of language, on the other hand, does not belong either to you or to me individually. It belongs to the language we are able to use which transcends our individuality (and thus, as Aquinas would argue, transcends our materiality, our bodily operations). My sensations may be *similar* to yours; my concepts or ideas are and have to be *identical* with yours – unless we are at cross-purposes, and that can easily be sorted out. It is for this reason that Aristotle and Aquinas insist that understanding, however much it needs a sensual concomitant, is not itself a sensual corporeal operation. For Aquinas it is not merely the acquisition of *new* ideas that depends on sense experience (we need sensual experience to interpret and talk about) but also every *use* of the concepts we have already acquired necessitates return to the *imaginatio* (imagination). Thinking, though not itself a bodily process, requires concomitant bodily processes. (That is why we think more clearly after a few drinks.)

Let us compare for a moment sensual desire or appetite which arises from sensual interpretation of the world with rational appetite or will which arises from rational interpretation of the world (or talking about it).

As I have often said before, a healthy and hungry dog confronted by a juicy steak interprets it as eminently edible and (unless trained in some way) cannot but try to get at it and eat it. (If it has been trained not to do so, it cannot but *not* do so.) Consider now *me*, equally healthy and hungry and confronted by the steak. I will of course share a version of the dog's sense-interpretation and desire, but I will also, as it were, talk to myself about the steak and tell myself that this steak belongs to someone else, that it is full of cholesterol, that it is the least efficient and most expensive way of acquiring protein ... and so on indefinitely. For talking or thinking can go on indefinitely; and this Aquinas thinks, and I do, is the root of human *freedom*: that there are limits to the operations of the nervous system, but no limits to talk. Rational desire is desiring something *under some description* and I can describe it in an indefinite number of ways.

To cut a long story short: I can make a *decision* about whether or not to eat the steak, and a decision is a complex dialectical interaction of the practical understanding and willing, all of which belong to the linguistic network, the deployment of words or concepts (which are the meaning of words). For this reason no non-linguistic animal can come to a *decision*.

It *will* do this rather than that, and sometimes it will hesitate before doing this rather than that, but it is not thinking and deciding; whatever it does is what it could not but do. It is because we have language that we can present ourselves with what is but might not be, with what is not but might be. For this reason we *move ourselves* in a more radical way than non-linguistic creatures: we are more animal than they are.

Now this capacity for free decision (not 'free will', but free *decision*, the fruit of both practical intelligence and willing) makes, as it seems to me, an absolute qualitative difference between linguistic and non-linguistic animals, and thus a difference between the social life of each.

Animals, of course, communicate with each other; and linguistic and non-linguistic animals also communicate with each other through the wondrous intricacy of sensitivity in the animal network of the nervous system. But *language* involves a new depth of communication between linguistic animals, and thus a new kind of society which is society in a new sense. It is based on language and this generates arts and skills and technology and traditions of understanding and history. Language produces the *city* as an extension of our bodily communication. And language gives rise to ethics which is more than ethology. Of course all sophisticated animals are equipped with inhibitions that restrain them (e.g. from attacking their young). And, as we have fairly recently come to understand, they live their lives within a highly specific complex pattern of behaviour; you might almost say a highly conventional behaviour pattern except that it is *not* conventional but genetically determined. There is a classical account by Konrad Lorentz of the wolf-fight. It is an absolutely serious and angry fight in which the combatants plainly seek to destroy each other. But, when the weaker wolf sees that he is losing, he makes a ritual gesture of submission and presents his unprotected throat to his adversary, who then is physically incapable of going for the kill. As Lorentz puts it: 'You can see he wants to but he can't.' It is easy to see how this instinct was developed by natural selection; it prevents the father wolf from killing his young in a rage. Wolves which were not programmed genetically in this way would have few surviving cubs so that their strain of gene would die out in the species.

We, of course, inherit many such instincts from our pre-linguistic ancestors. And this is a valuable inheritance indeed. Pope John Paul II seems to think that it is the profound intuitive basis of morality. But it is wholly inadequate to cope with the world which humans have created because of language and technology. If you were made to put a baby on the fire to kill it, you would be revolted and probably physically sick (this is the old ethological inheritance in you). But if they put you in an airplane and made you press the button to release napalm on the village below, you are, of course, having exactly the same effect on the babies there. Yet, while you would, I hope, vigorously disapprove, you might not have an instinctive physical reaction, just because you are so far away and cannot see what you are doing. Behaviour that is the *fruit* of language needs to be *controlled* by language, by reason. We need ethics.

This means that our kind of social living demands the deliberate cultivation of certain dispositions which will sustain social friendship. It needs the virtues. These have to be cultivated by education. We are not born with them. In order to acquire them we need education in its true broad sense. We also need laws. Both virtues and laws imply a *citizenship*. Neither the notion of laws nor virtues nor morality makes any sense outside the linguistic rational society. And the same must be true of rights and duties. No non-linguistic animal can have a duty or right, for example to vote. It cannot be a citizen of a linguistic society. Our critique of the mistreatment of our fellow-animals should not, as it seems to me, be intrinsically legalistic. But the survival of human society demands *virtues* even more than it demands *laws*. Indeed, for Aristotle, it demands virtues without which there could be no laws. Human society, the *polis*, he thinks, is based on *philia*, political friendship which involves being concerned for the happiness and flourishing and, therefore, the virtues of others. And important virtues are gentleness, and compassion and related dispositions. It is because we have lost sight of the *political* significance of *such* virtues of temperateness that we speak of animal *rights*, as though pretending that animals were citizens. We can, of course, demand by *law* that citizens be educated to cultivate gentleness and shun cruelty, just as we can demand by law that they learn to read and write and know about physics.

Saying that animals have rights in law is a little like saying that books have a right in law to be read, and music to be enjoyed, and that the left side of the road has a right to be driven on. Such things as education are a necessary part of the peace and flourishing of citizens, and it is only in modern liberal times that people have suggested that the state should have no concern with them. I think that is a regrettable muddle.

Index

A page number followed by 'n' plus number indicates a footnote.

INDEX

INDEX

Made in United States
North Haven, CT
23 August 2022